UNQUALIFIED:

The Ineligible Bachelor

Lomasi Laine

Copyright © 2022 by Lomasi Laine

All rights reserved. In accordance with the US Copyright Act of 1976, the scanning, uploading, and electronic sharing of any part of this book without the permission of the author constitutes unlawful piracy and theft of the author's intellectual property. If you would like to use material from the book (other than for review purposes), prior written permission must be obtained by contacting the author. Thank you for your support of the author's rights.

Text: Lomasi Laine
Cover Design: Jennifer Stimson
Interior Design and Layout: Danielle Smith-Boldt

ISBNs:
979-8-9863673-4-7 (Paperback)
979-8-9863673-0-9 (eBook)

To my circle of strong women and prayer warriors,
who listened, interceded, prayed with me and counseled.

To the loves of my life and biggest cheerleaders:

My son, my heart, your loyalty, wisdom and intuition
are incredible.

My "big little sister" who always has an ear
to listen and heart to care.

Pie, who taught me to seek the Lord in His Word
and pray in all situations.

And finally, Mommy, who always forewarned me
that "he is not the one" and to "pray on it".

Table of Contents

Introduction vii

Ineligible Bachelor #1:
Mr. Fora Season 1

Ineligible Bachelor #2:
Mr. Fora New Season 13

Ineligible Bachelor #3:
Mr. Iam Ready 21

Ineligible Bachelor #4:
Mr. Pho Bia 35

Ineligible Bachelor #5:
Mr. Wido Wer 55

Ineligible Bachelor #6:
Mr. Dawaitis Over 85

Ineligible Bachelor #7:
Mr. Prince Charming 129

Ineligible Bachelor #8:
Mr. Recen Lee Divorced Part I 137

Ineligible Bachelor #9:
Mr. Recen Lee Divorced Part II 147

Epilogue 157
Scriptures 163
Self Reflection 167

Introduction

If you are reading this book, you've probably dated some ineligible bachelors in your lifetime. If you are currently dating one, then you may be trying to figure out what is wrong with you or what you have done wrong. If any of the bachelors in this book resonate with you, then I am here to tell you, IT'S NOT YOU! Believe him when he says, "It's not you, it's me."

It has taken me over twenty years—dating several ineligible bachelors, marrying two husbands, and learning what God had to teach me about myself, my worth, and my value—to obtain this mindset: these men were not qualified! They were not qualified to love ME.

One of the definitions of "unqualified" is not fit or lacking, as in unqualified for the job. When I looked at synonyms, the two that stood out to me were "incapable" and "ineligible." So, there you have it ladies, the title of this book, *Unqualified: The Ineligible Bachelor.*

While doing my research, I looked up the antonyms for unqualified and noticed the word "suitable." That word made me think of a Bible verse I read several years ago that is engraved on my heart. In Genesis 2:18 (NLT), God says, "It is not good for the man to be alone. I will make a helper **suitable** for him." If God made me suitable for a man, then surely, he should be suitable for me. At least that's my take on it!

This book describes different types of ineligible bachelors I have dated (and married). Please join me as I share my journey full of teachable moments. Although some were painful, I believe God allowed me to go through these events so I could encourage other women in similar situations and help turn their ashes into beauty.

I believe ultimately the eligible bachelor is out there looking for me, that special man suitable for me. God says I am a treasure! His word says, "The man who **finds** a wife finds a **treasure,** and he receives favor from the Lord." (Proverbs 18:22, NLT) *We* are treasures, ladies! I don't know about you, but I believe a treasure can be found only by the one who is qualified to find it. Oh, sure, several people can be on the hunt for the treasure, but it doesn't mean they are equipped to find it. If they do find it, they won't know what to do with it, won't be able to appreciate it, or they won't understand the true purpose of it.

The word of God also says, "Who can find a virtuous and capable wife? She is more precious than rubies." (Proverbs 31:10, NLT) I am more precious than rubies! And The Message translation says diamonds! **We are worth more than rubies and diamonds!** And God calls us capable (qualified), so I know He has a man qualified for each one of us!

This book is not about male bashing nor is it about shaming anyone I have dated or married. They were all great men with unique qualities and were very special to me at a specific time in my life. I am still friends

Introduction

with some of them ... well, at least until this book gets published. I'm kidding! On that note, names, places, and physical descriptions have been changed to protect individuals' privacy.

This book is for women who wonder if they did "too much or not enough to be loved." Through my physical, mental, emotional, and spiritual experiences—and the joys and many pains I encountered along the way—I pray you are able to use this book to identify men who are ineligible to love *you*. Whether you are examining past relationships or current ones, stopping a cycle or preventing one, God does have an eligible bachelor for you. Will you trust him enough to let the ineligible bachelor go? You are the treasure worth finding!

Ineligible Bachelor #1:
Mr. Fora Season

"Excuse me ma'am, today is your lucky day!" a female flight attendant said as I sat in my window seat of an early flight departing Los Angeles International Airport. "There's a gentleman who wants to know if you want to come sit in first class?"

Here we were, twenty minutes into the flight, and now this. I wasn't taking her seriously. I didn't know anyone on that flight, and no one knew me. Being scammed was not on my morning agenda.

"Me?" I asked, looking at her skeptically. "I don't know anyone on this flight, miss. So, umm ... no thanks."

I arranged my pillow and blanket and prepared to get some sleep after being up all night. After all, it was going to be a seven-hour-plus flight. As I was drifting off, I heard a man's voice ask, "Is anyone sitting here?"

Out the corner of my right eye, I saw a medium, brown-skinned man with short wavy hair and a thick mustache (Steve Harvey thick) leaning over to me. Although I didn't know him, I recognized him. I had engaged in light conversation with him in line at the airport while boarding our flight to Rhode Island.

"May I sit next to you? We had such a great conversation in line, I would like to continue talking to you."

"Oh, hi," I said with a dubious chuckle. "No. No one's sitting here. I don't mind," I said, putting down the armrest. To be honest, I kind of did because I was so tired.

I know what you are thinking: he was a stranger, could've been crazy, and all of that. Yes, I know! And yes, my mom taught me about "stranger danger," but it didn't feel weird because of our conversation in the airport. This happened over twenty years ago, and I wouldn't entertain this nowadays with all the human sex trafficking ploys.

The gentleman sat down and buckled his seat belt. I was really intrigued by his youthful skin but distracted by his mustache. I couldn't help but wonder about his age. His smooth, pretty skin glowed and made him look youthful, but the mustache made him appear rather old. It looked like one of those fake mustaches they sell in the Halloween shops. I was waiting for it to fall off.

"Hi, I'm Jeffrey," he introduced himself. "What's your name?"

"Hi, my name is Lomasi."

While Jeffrey and I were getting acquainted, the same flight attendant who asked me about sitting in first class excitedly walked over.

"This is the gentleman I was talking about!" she interrupted. "He's so kind. Since you wouldn't sit in first

Mr. Fora Season

class, he gave up his seat to an elderly woman so he could come to the back and sit next to you!"

"What!? Are you serious?" I asked, gaping at him and then back at the flight attendant. I was in shock because we literally had a five-minute conversation in line at the gate. He seemed like a nice guy and was funny, but there was no initial "spark," at least not for me. I certainly wouldn't have predicted it would lead to a seat change from first class and a six-and-a-half-hour conversation later.

He asked about my trip and what brought me to Los Angeles. I told him I had come to Long Beach to take a test teachers must pass to work in California public schools. I explained I was a teacher from Boston (Worcester to be exact) and I was strongly considering relocating to the Los Angeles area.

He told me he was in L.A. scouting basketball players. At that time, I had no interest in sports and no idea what "scouting" meant. I didn't even bother to ask. We discussed our children—my eight-year-old son and his son who was twelve. We talked and laughed about so many things that the time passed quickly.

When we landed in Rhode Island, he grabbed his black carry-on that had an interesting emblem of a bear on it and we exited the plane. We exchanged numbers before I headed to baggage claim and he to his connecting gate.

The next day, when I got in from work, I received a call from a flower shop. They needed my address so they could make a delivery. The following day, I received a dozen beautiful pink roses. The card with the flowers read, "It was really nice talking to you.—Jeffrey Ball." Now the gentleman from the plane had piqued my interest!

"Did you receive the flowers?" he asked, when he called me later that evening. "Hope you like them."

"Yes, I did. Thank you so much! They're beautiful!" I assured him, looking at them on the dining room table and smiling.

We talked on the phone every day after that, getting to know one another; we laughed so much and really enjoyed our conversations. He was ten years older than I, but we shared the same birth month, and his birthday was four days after mine. I told him I was a professional dancer (in addition to being a teacher), had done some musicals, and had traveled to New York often for dance classes. I learned that he was a scout for an NBA team. At that point, the emblem I saw on his carry-on flashed in my mind and the conversation we had on the plane about "scouting basketball players" made sense.

About a week later, we made plans for him to come visit for a weekend in Worcester. He wanted to spend time with me, accompany me to my sorority sister's wedding, meet and take my family to dinner, as well as do some scouting at a well-known college in Massachusetts (ironically, the same college my little sister was attending at the time). In the four days he was planning to be there, we had a packed schedule. Jeffrey sent me his itinerary and was scheduled to arrive that Friday.

I met him at the airport, and he rented a car for the weekend. It was at the car rental counter I noticed he had two cell phones. He explained one was for business and the other for personal use. I didn't think more about it, although he used them pretty frequently that weekend.

Mr. For a Season

We drove to his hotel so he could get settled and then headed to dinner with my family. He met my mom, a former probation officer and a true mama bear, who could sense somebody's B.S. immediately. Next was my stepdad, a criminal defense attorney; he would ask all the right questions, sift through the B.S., and what he was not able to find out, his private investigator, Moe, would finish.

Dinner with my stepdad, mom, and son, Chris, was a hit. We laughed and talked the whole time. I really wanted Jeffrey to meet my biological dad, but he was in Myrtle Beach for a golf tournament. Since my dad was still bitter from the divorce and my mother's remarriage, he wouldn't have joined us for dinner anyway. I would have had to arrange a separate meeting.

That weekend Jeffrey went with me to the wedding in Providence, Rhode Island. We had a great time and danced a lot. He was thoughtful and attentive the entire time; he was the perfect date.

On our final day together, he invited me to go with him to the university where he would be scouting basketball players. It was exciting although I didn't really understand the game.

After the practice, my sister came to the sports center and met Jeffrey. She knew more about sports than I did so she was excited to meet him.

Unqualified: The Ineligible Bachelor

It was official: he made a huge impression on my family and ended up developing a friendship with my stepdad.

Jeffrey and I spent a lot of our dating time on the phone. That weekend was technically our first time together since our conversation on the plane. I felt comfortable around him and enjoyed his company. Our relationship was developing into something special pretty fast.

"If you had to design the perfect diamond ring, what would it look like?" he randomly asked one day.

"I want a jade and diamond ring."

"How does that go together?" he asked, sounding confused. "I mean, jade and a diamond?"

"Yes! And it looks so amazing together!" I told him, trying to convince him of my perfect wedding ring. "I saw this nail technician at the salon with a jade and diamond ring, but it had yellow gold. I only wear white gold so that's what I want instead."

"You want a jade and diamond ring with white gold?" Jeffrey asked, sarcastically. "How about platinum? It is heavier than white gold," he explained. "I don't know about this creative idea of yours. Let me call my jeweler and see if it can be done." He immediately got on the phone with his jeweler who confirmed it was possible.

From that moment on, we talked about wedding rings and a car he wanted to buy me. He talked about blueprints of a house to be built—and we had just met a few weeks earlier! I hadn't even thought about my plans to move to Los Angeles. After all, that was where I met Jeffrey.

Mr. For a Season

To be honest, I found it interesting that the house blueprints showed it being built in the Atlanta, Georgia, area. My family and friends knew moving to Atlanta had been a dream of mine for several years. I even had made plans to move there with a close friend until one day God woke me up to the word, *California*.

When I had told my friend I was moving to Los Angeles instead of Atlanta, he stopped talking to me until we reconnected on Facebook nine years later. Now, here I was entertaining the idea of a ring and a house in Atlanta with a man I just met. *Hmm … maybe I heard God wrong.*

I told my stepdad about the blueprints, but he had already seen them because Jeffrey came to him first. Now it all made sense! They had been having conversations on a regular basis since they met.

But I really needed to have this conversation with my dad. I was a daddy's girl, and he was very protective. I knew he wasn't going to let this man come in and sweep his daughter off her feet before he even met Jeffrey. Apparently, I needed to make this next step happen sooner than later.

On October 31, Halloween night, I took my son trick-or-treating. We stopped by his grandparents' house to show off his costume and get candy before we went home for the night. Plus, my stepdad was adamant that I come by because he had something "worth my attention" to give me.

He was grinning ear to ear when he handed me a black box; I looked at my stepdad apprehensively. He assured me it was okay and told me to open it. Inside was a beautiful platinum necklace with a platinum and diamond cross—from Jeffrey. He had it shipped to my stepdad's office.

I was speechless. He totally caught me off guard this time because everything else he had said he wanted to buy or send I respectfully declined with "No, thank you." For some reason, this necklace seemed special, and I chose to keep it.

At 4 a.m. November 1, the phone woke me up. We all know it's bad news when you get a call that time of morning.

"Hey, hon, it's Sarah (my cousin). I know it is early in the morning. I just wanted to call and tell you your dad had a heart attack this morning and was rushed to Saint Vincent's Hospital."

"Oh, my God! I'm on my way!" I anxiously responded.

I called my mother and told her the news and within twenty minutes she was there to pick up my son and me. Before I left home, I grabbed the cross from Jeffrey and put it around my neck. We dropped Chris off with my stepfather and continued to the hospital. I was numb and in shock, but I knew to pray. I put my hand on my chest and held on to the cross because I felt I needed Jesus now more than ever.

My two aunts were sitting in the waiting room when I arrived. I prayed alone and together with them. A doctor spoke to us about next steps and asked medical history questions to see if my dad would qualify for a heart transplant. Shortly after, my aunt and I were allowed to see him.

My dad was hooked up to several machines and fighting for his life. Although he didn't appear coherent, he was thrashing his arms around. I don't know if he was literally fighting because he did not like all those wires connected to him, or if he was upset his daughter was seeing him in this traumatic setting. He continued to pound his fists on the bed as his eyes met mine. I began praying out loud holding on to my cross even tighter.

A family friend had driven to my sister's college and brought her to the hospital. When she arrived, I was on the phone talking to my job and giving them an update. My aunts surrounded her and inquired about college life.

Just then, I saw the doctor go into the waiting room with my aunts and uncles and close the door. Moments later, my blood ran cold when I heard my uncle scream. I immediately hung up the phone. My whole body froze. My daddy had died.

I had enough mental capacity to quickly call Jeffrey, who had been checking on me throughout the morning, to tell him my dad had died. He caught the next flight out and arrived that evening. I struggled with how to tell my son that his Grampy, whom he loved so much and spent time with every week, was gone. He would no longer be here to take Chris to eat, to the park to ride his bike, or to the driving range. I was at a loss for words. Jeffrey comforted and assured me that he would be by my side.

We took my son to dinner later that evening. Jeffrey helped me explain to Chris about his Grampy. I'll never

Unqualified: The Ineligible Bachelor

forget how creatively he did it. He used the movie, *The Lion King,* as an example (which happened to be my son's favorite movie since he was two years old). Jeffrey described the relationship between Simba and Mufasa and connected it to my son and his grandfather. He said when Mufasa unexpectedly died, Simba was sad and mad, and that was okay.

Following Jeffrey's lead, I told Chris that Grampy had unexpectedly died. Jeffrey went back to the movie analogy talking about how Simba would always have his dad, Mufasa, and the memories they shared in his heart. Those memories helped Simba take his rightful place as king when he got older. Likewise, Chris would always have his Grampy and their memories in his heart, and he would one day take his rightful place as head of the family when he got older.

"It's the 'circle of life,'" Jeffrey quoted.

It was such a beautiful analogy and my son received it well. I was so grateful, and over twenty years later, I still am.

Being the oldest daughter, I had to make funeral arrangements with the help of my aunts. Jeffrey offered to pay for the funeral, but it wasn't necessary. He wanted to help in some way, so mom suggested he buy a shirt for my dad to wear. So that's what he did. As we waited for family members to arrive from out of town, Jeffrey had to head back to work.

Little did I know, that would be the last time I saw Jeffrey. Just like that, he was gone. For the longest time, I thought he was an angel. It wasn't until several weeks later, when things began to settle, that I understood *why*

Mr. For a Season

God sent him into my life. It was for this specific season. Even though Jeffrey had all these plans and ideas for a future with me, they were not God's plans; therefore, he was ineligible.

"For everything there is a season, a time for every activity under heaven. A time to embrace and a time to turn away." (Ecclesiastes 3:1, 5b, NLT)

Ineligible Bachelor #2:
Mr. Fora New Season

It was just three weeks after returning from Los Angeles and meeting Jeffrey that my dad passed. As I began my journey of grief, I decided I wasn't moving to L.A. Honestly, my dad had not wanted me to move to the West Coast because I didn't have any family or friends there. He was worried that if something happened to me or his grandchild no one would be able to help us. I wanted to honor his feelings now more than ever. I began adjusting to my new normal … life without Daddy.

I hadn't dated anyone since my relationship with Jeffrey ended. I just focused on my emotional and mental health and taking care of my son. Chris and I spent more time around my mom and stepdad, especially because my son now feared losing his other grandparents. All the major holidays were tough for us: the first Thanksgiving, Christmas, and New Year's without my dad.

Normally, my son, sister, and I would go to my grandmother's house and spend time with Daddy on those holidays. We tried to keep up with visiting our grandmother and other family members on these holidays and reminisce about my dad, but it became difficult for my sister to continue to visit.

Around late spring, I decided to attend a huge educational recruitment fair in Boston with my uncle. He was a school psychologist and was looking to work in a different school system located in another state.

While my uncle was "working the room," a gentleman approached me about my credentials and potentially working in his school district. I told him I wasn't there to look for employment but only there to support my uncle.

"Are you in education?" he asked.

"Yes, I am a teacher," I nonchalantly responded. Like I said, I was not interested in relocating at the time. I tried looking around at other booths without being rude.

"Oh, what do you teach?" he continued.

"I teach middle school Spanish."

"Are you sure you wouldn't be interested in coming to work in my school district?" he inquired again. "We have a large Spanish-speaking population and could really use you on our team."

"No, sorry. I'm not looking to relocate currently, but thank you anyway."

"How about this. Why don't you come out to visit the schools and see if you like the district," he suggested.

"What's the name of your school district?" I asked.

"Compton Unified School District."

"Compton? As in Compton, California?" I asked. "Please excuse my ignorance, but I don't know anything about Compton except for what I've seen in the movies—and it seems pretty rough."

He laughed and said, "Let's arrange for you to come visit so you can see for yourself. Fill out the application, and I will have someone from human resources contact you and arrange a tour."

So, there it was. I was being offered another opportunity when I wasn't looking for one—in California ... again. My uncle walked over and joined the conversation. He encouraged me to visit Compton and told me he would come with me. I decided to fill out the application. *You could always say no,* I told myself. HR contacted me about a week later and arranged a visit around Memorial Day weekend.

My uncle and I flew to Los Angeles and that visit was life changing. I visited Compton and was so happy I did; it wasn't what I had imagined. I visited a middle school and two elementary schools. I was offered jobs by all three principals. The school district offered to give me an emergency teaching credential, which meant I had one year to finish taking the test to teach in California schools.

While I was there, my uncle and I viewed some apartments in a city about 25 minutes away to get an idea of rental prices. I called several apartment managers and left messages, but no one called me back. I ended up in one complex praying to God in the middle of the courtyard. I reminded him that he put California in my spirit the year before. I told him I didn't know what to do, and I needed him to guide me.

We walked to the next building. A Hispanic woman was standing out front, and I discovered she was the building manager. I inquired about vacant units, and she told me she wouldn't have any until mid-July. My uncle asked if it would be possible to see a unit because I was heading back to Boston the next day. She arranged with a tenant for me to take a look.

It was then she told me she would hold the apartment for me on a $100 money order deposit until I moved in August. A $100 deposit to hold an apartment from June to August!? No problem. That was all God, and he answered my prayer!

Chris and I moved to California the beginning of August. We had about a month to get settled before our new normal kicked in. A new city for us, a new job for me, a new school for him, and new friends. *Yikes! What did I do?* I asked myself one day. *How did I take this kid away from what he knew most—his family and friends—and uproot him 3,000-plus miles away? Especially after losing his grandfather. Am I a bad parent?* I was overcome with anxiety. *Jesus, take the wheel.*

One evening in early October, my stepdad called and said he received an interesting call from someone asking for my number. They were trying to contact me, but the phone number they had was disconnected. He told the caller I had moved to California, but he would ask my permission to give them my number. When I asked him who it was, I was in complete shock! A few days later, my cell phone rang displaying an unknown number.

"Hello?" I asked, hesitantly.

"Hi, Lomasi! How are you? How's little man?" asked a voice I recognized. "I have been trying to get in contact

Mr. For a New Season

with you! I had to call your dad to get your information. I see you finally made it to California."

"Hey, Jeffrey!" I screamed. I was so happy to hear from him. We hadn't talked in almost a year. It felt good to be in this new city and hear a familiar voice—especially one I wasn't expecting to ever hear again.

"My son is good, adjusting to the move," I replied.

"Hey, I'll be in Los Angeles for a few days. I want to see you and little man and catch up on things," he announced. "When can you meet? I have to visit a high school and watch a player tomorrow, but I am free for dinner."

"Okay, tomorrow will be great!" I accepted. "I can't wait to tell Chris. He's going to be so excited!"

"Meet me at my hotel and then we can go grab some dinner," he said, and proceeded to give me the information.

"All right, see you tomorrow. Can't wait to catch up!" I said, feeling excited.

Wow, maybe God is bringing us back together. Just like he brought back the California opportunity. Maybe I had to get through the loss of my dad and this move before anything serious could really happen. My mind began whirling about all the possibilities.

The next evening, Chris and I met Jeffrey at his hotel. When I saw him, it seemed so nostalgic. We were all happy to be together again, and Chris remembered who he was. But although Jeffrey was familiar, something felt different. The hour we sat in his hotel room catching up, he must have answered almost every call on both cell phones. *Ah, the two cell phones,* I quickly remembered. It was somewhat tolerable before, but now it was just annoying!

Unqualified: The Ineligible Bachelor

This was the first time I was turned off by Jeffrey. I was expecting him to be more attentive and engaged since we hadn't seen or talked to each other in a year. Some of the calls weren't even business related; they sounded like he was talking to his friends.

As it started to get later, I told him I needed to feed my son. Jeffrey decided to cut his last phone conversation short, and we headed to the restaurant. Of course, Chris enjoyed himself because he got to order whatever he wanted off the menu. While eating and attempting to carry on a conversation, Jeffrey continued to answer both phones, which rang constantly. It was like Wall Street! I think at one point he was even talking to his sister! It was then I decided this second-chance meeting was a second-chance flop. This was not going to work.

When I dropped him off at his hotel, he made a comment about getting back together and all these other plans. I had to really think and ask myself the tough questions. Did he stay on his phones like this before? Heck, no! Jeffrey was trying to impress me by putting his best foot forward. He had courted me. But was this my future if we had stayed together and eventually gotten married? Tonight was far from courting and definitely not his best effort.

I actually felt like a charity case. He made a mediocre impression on me this time. I decided a future with Jeffrey wasn't going to happen. He was too busy for me. It was so obvious who and what his priorities were—and I was not one of them.

He was ineligible. Mr. Fora Season, who I thought was Mr. New Season, was now Mr. No Season. That was the last time I saw or talked to Jeffrey. I decided I was going to take a chance and put my eggs in a different basket.

"No, dear brothers and sisters, I have not achieved it, but I focus on this one thing: Forgetting the past and looking forward to what lies ahead."
(Philippians 3:13, NLT)

Ineligible Bachelor #3:
Mr. Iam Ready

My family and I were staying at a hotel in Los Angeles waiting for my furniture and car to arrive from Boston. The sister of one of my friends invited me to lunch and the soul food restaurant just happened to be across the street from my hotel. I decided to go just to get out of the hotel room for a few hours.

Tonya, my friend's sister, and I were talking, laughing, and getting to know each other when Mr. Iam Ready appeared on the scene. I've never seen so much confidence exude from one person! When Tonya stepped away from the booth, Mr. Iam Ready, a friend of hers, eased into her seat and slid a napkin over to me with some chicken-scratch writing on it.

"So, you gon' be my girlfriend. Here's my number. Call me so we can go out some time," he said, in a southern, pimpish-sounding voice as he winked at me. The napkin read: 310-336-9336, Earl. Now, I wasn't trying to be mean, but I had literally just landed in L.A. the day before. The last thing on my mind was having a boyfriend. I didn't even know where my furniture was!

"Eh, no. No, thank you." (That was my modus operandi, otherwise known as MO, when I wasn't interested in something or someone. Kill 'em with kindness.) "I just landed yesterday. I'm not interested in dating anyone at this time," I explained. "I haven't even moved into my apartment and gotten settled yet!"

"Oh, is that right? Okay. Well, we can be friends then," Earl insisted.

I chuckled and rolled my eyes and thought, *this guy is something else.* And friends is what we became—initially.

Two weeks had passed since my furniture arrived. Tonya happened to call to see how we were settling in our new apartment and asked if I needed any help.

"Yes! Tonya would you be able to help me set up my bed this weekend? I've been sleeping on just my mattress for a couple of weeks."

"I'm so sorry, Lomasi. I won't be able to. I just started taking classes and have to work on a paper. Why don't you ask Earl? I know he would love to help," she said, giggling. "Here is his number. Tell him I gave you his number and told you to call him."

I hadn't spoken to Earl since we met, and he "slid" his number to me. After all, I did explain to him that I wanted to get settled. *He should understand. Right?* Hmm, this was definitely going to be awkward. But I dialed his number anyway.

"Hello?"

"Hey, Earl!" I greeted him. "This is Lomasi, Tonya's friend."

Mr. Iam Ready

"Yeah, what's happening?" he asked in that pimpish-sounding voice again.

"I got your number from Tonya and she said you would be able to help me with something."

"Oh, is that right? Tonya said I could help you?" he asked, sarcastically. "What you need?"

"Can you help me put my bed together?"

"You need me to help you with your bed?" Earl asked, laughing.

"Yes," I responded, but soon realized we were on two different pages.

In a low "sexy" voice, Earl asked, "What kind of help do you need with 'your bed?'"

At that point I was embarrassed and tried to clean it all up. After we got through the comedy, Earl said he would come over to my apartment and help me. That was the start of our friendship. I eventually helped him on some business projects he had as well.

After about three months, our friendship turned into dating. I remember our first date to the Hollywood Casino. The lounge was hosting karaoke night, and I was blown away by people's talent! They were amazing! It seemed like everyone there was trying to get a record deal.

And any thoughts about my participating (regardless of how much alcohol I'd had) weren't happening at all—period. So much for doing karaoke for the fun of it. That went out of the window when a gentleman got up and sang *Superstar/Until You Come Back to Me* by Luther Vandross. We had a really good time. Earl was a funny guy and made me laugh all night.

Unqualified: The Ineligible Bachelor

I remember our first Christmas together. We met at Tonya's house a few days before Christmas and did a gift exchange because my son and I were traveling to Boston to be with my family for the holidays. Earl and I agreed on how many items we would buy each other. I don't remember all the gifts we exchanged, but I do remember he bought me a two-way pager, which was high tech and expensive at the time. (Yes! A two-way pager. I took it way back!) He spent way over the gift budget we had set, but I was so excited and grateful.

When I returned from Boston, we continued to date and enjoy spending time with each other. I supported him with his business endeavors. One morning, shortly after the new year, something traumatic happened.

"Earl, someone just ran into the back of my car, and I cannot move my neck!" I cried out in pain.

"Did you get the driver's information? Call the police?" Earl asked.

"No," I winced. "The woman hit me from behind, came to my car window, and asked me to pull over to some side street. She asked me if I was okay, but I couldn't move or respond so she wrote her information on a paper and drove away." I was crying at this point.

"Where are you?" Earl asked.

"I don't know!" I sobbed. I really didn't know because I was still unfamiliar with the area. I started to panic.

"Look around. Do you see a street sign? Does anything look familiar to you?"

"I can't move my neck!" I shouted in panic and frustration. I didn't know why Earl was asking me questions to answers I had already given him. It was annoying, and it wasn't helping the situation.

"I don't know why you called me," Earl replied. "Call 911."

I don't know why you called me? Did he really ask that question when I was just seriously hurt in an accident? I didn't know where I was and was all alone! I wanted him to come to my rescue. Damn! I knew he wasn't going to ride in on a white horse with shining armor, but I needed help, fool!

I hung up with Earl and dialed 911. The operator asked me for my location and of course I could not tell him. All I could provide him with was the major street I was initially driving down. I explained that I came to a red light and got hit from the back. I also told him what I remembered passing along the way.

I was so scared because I had never been involved in something so serious and had to fend for myself. *Maybe this was what Daddy meant when he tried to get me to change my mind about moving to California. I had no family to help me and my so-called boyfriend asked me why I called him. Did I truly make the wrong decision moving here?* All these questions ran through my head as I was waiting for the paramedics to arrive. I was so relieved when they found me.

Unqualified: The Ineligible Bachelor

They took me to the nearest hospital, and I waited to be seen. Eventually I called Earl and told him the name of the hospital I was in. When he saw me, he began laughing as if to say "what a hot mess." I don't know what was so damn funny, but apparently, he got a kick out of it.

Again, I don't know what I was expecting from him, but jokes were not on my list. After spending a few hours there with me, I asked him to pick up Chris from school after they discharged me.

The next day we picked up my car so it wouldn't get towed. I also had to follow up with my primary care doctor. He placed me on a four-week leave from work due to the pain I was suffering and possible head trauma. Earl came by my apartment almost every day to check on me.

Over the next few months, our relationship encountered some peaks and valleys. Earl and I had clashing opinions on how I should raise my son. According to Earl, I "babied him." I disagreed. Chris was nine years old, and I was his mother, his only family—his only sense of normalcy. Everyone else was back East. The last traumatic event he weathered was the loss of his Grampy. Here he was thousands of miles away from his family, and his mom had been in a serious accident.

Mr. Iam Ready

Deep down, I knew he worried about losing me too, and this situation didn't help ease his mind. I was trying to make him feel as comfortable as possible with this move and the major adjustments he was being forced to make. It was around this time I began detecting some resentment on Earl's part toward my son. He hadn't spent a lot of time around both of us like he did while I was recovering. Earl knew I was a package deal. I wasn't sure if he was truly ready or capable of dealing with that.

That summer, Chris and I went back East during summer vacation to visit our family. I knew he needed to see his grandparents, auntie, dad, and friends. Honestly, I needed to see my family and friends too. This trip back home really rejuvenated us. After a month, we headed back to California to prepare for the new school year.

In September, my birthday month, my alarm went off and I woke up listening to *The Steve Harvey Morning Show*. Then the craziest thing happened. I heard a phone ringing on the air and, simultaneously, my phone started ringing in my bedroom. I answered the phone and the next thing I knew, Steve Harvey was asking for me and telling me to wake up.

He told me someone there had something to say to me. I was tripping because I didn't have a clue as to who it could be. I thought maybe it was my family surprising me for my birthday. The next voice I heard was Earl's! He started talking about how he loved me and wanted me in his life. Then he proposed! At the same time, Chris came walking into my room holding a case with a beautiful diamond ring! I couldn't believe it! He definitely surprised me!

Unqualified: The Ineligible Bachelor

I was overjoyed and said yes. After Earl's proposal and my response, Steve Harvey cracked some jokes about my son holding on to the diamond ring all night and then congratulated us on our engagement. It was so surreal!

How in the heck did my son keep this diamond ring and the plan a secret? How long had he known? This kid usually can't hold water, but he surprised the heck out of his mommy that morning! Earl's proposal was so creative. The special part of it all was he included my son! Maybe he was ready to accept me as a package deal after all.

Earl and I talked to our family and friends about the engagement for the next month or so. We began discussing wedding plans and selected a wedding date. I knew I wanted to get married by water, but I didn't want to have a typical beach wedding, so we started scouting locations that weren't "beachy." We found the perfect place in San Pedro.

Next on the list was joining an eight-week premarital class at his church. This is where some of the red flags began to surface and get exposed. They were not the typical flags like making a pact to remain celibate before the wedding (we were already a celibate couple), having a financial conversation to discuss assets and debts, age difference (he was ten years older than I was) or even becoming "one." Some problems that surfaced were related to childhood trauma.

Things that happened to me or I witnessed as a young girl shaped my view of marriage and the expectations of me as a wife and him as a husband. Our premarital mentors asked Earl if he understood the "what and why" of my mindset due to the trauma. They asked if he was willing to accept me knowing this information. He claimed he understood and could accept me, but he laughed and made light of it. He also said he was just "ready to get married."

Over the next few weeks, we had some really intense discussions in the couple's counseling sessions. So much so that our mentors recommended we not get married until we revisited "why" we were getting married, read some Christian marital books on being set free from darkness, and continued with extended counseling sessions.

Hindsight is 20/20 and we should've ended it there and walked away, but we tried to do what was suggested in the name of love. I believe God was trying early on to spare us the hurt, anger, bitterness, and pain that was to come.

A few months passed, and Chris and I traveled back East during the Christmas holiday. While I was there, I had lunch with a close friend who asked me about my engagement and future husband. She asked me one question that stopped me dead in my tracks—and made me question my feelings immediately.

"Do you love him?"

I froze. *Do I love him?* I whispered to myself. About thirty seconds later, my friend said I took too long to respond and suggested I rethink my decision. *Why did I*

Unqualified: The Ineligible Bachelor

have a hard time answering that question? I know I love him. Why did it take me so long to answer? Was I really in love with him? All these questions flooded my mind that day and the days following. I decided to break off the engagement.

I flew back to Los Angeles knowing I needed to have a conversation with Earl as soon as possible. I told him what I was experiencing—all the questions and feelings that were surfacing. I explained that I thought it best to break off our engagement. It was a difficult decision, but one that I had to make. The grieving over the next month was tough, I can't lie. I tried my best not to call him and allow my heart to heal.

A few weeks later, I found out my school district was going to lay off teachers come June due to the new No Child Left Behind Act imposed by President George W. Bush. I began preparing early and started looking for apartments that were cheaper to live in so I could make ends meet during the summer months. I made phone calls to various property management companies daily.

My first call was a two-bedroom apartment that would slash my rent almost in half. The property manager gave me the address and told me to come view the apartment later that day. The address seemed very familiar. When I arrived, I knew why. It was Earl's apartment building! I called Earl and asked if he knew which unit was vacant. He told me he would find out. When I met the property manager and walked through the courtyard, Earl came out to join us. It was my first time seeing him since the breakup. The property manager walked me to the unit; it was directly across from Earl's apartment! At that point, all we could do was laugh. Like usual, Earl made a joke out of it.

Mr. Iam Ready

I ended up moving into the apartment about a month later. The move is what brought Earl and me back together—we thought it was fate. We married three weeks later. Nothing fancy, just us, Chris, two witnesses, and a pastor from his church in a small, chapel-like room.

"What God has brought together, let no man put asunder," declared the minister.

The iciest chill went through my body. *Maybe it's cold feet,* I thought. *But I should be happy and excited,* I argued with myself. *You can do this, Lomasi. You're just nervous and it's normal. No! Just say, no and end this,* I vacillated. I wanted to run, but I was stuck—emotionally and physically.

"Do you take this man to be your wedded husband, to have and to hold, from this day forward, for better, for worse, for richer or poorer, in sickness and health, to love and to cherish, 'til death do you part?"

All I could say was, "I do."

Over the next few years, the union was tumultuous. Earl became controlling and our marriage was filled with deception, physical and verbal aggression, and assault by both of us including my son. Don't get me wrong. Every day wasn't bad, but most days were not good.

My mom, stepdad, and sister had relocated to Las Vegas, and I took off to visit them every chance I could

Unqualified: The Ineligible Bachelor

get to have peace. The next step for us was separation. And I really needed it for my sanity. We went to marital counseling. We started to see a breakthrough, light at the end of the tunnel. The stipulation for him to move back home was that he needed to go to individual therapy for at least six sessions followed by family therapy sessions so Chris could be included in fixing the broken family unit.

Earl agreed to individual therapy, but he was unwilling to attend family counseling with Chris and me. That was devastating. That letdown, along with one more blow up, landed me at a paralegal's office filing for divorce. I said this before and I'll say it again: hindsight is 20/20 and we should've ended it in the premarital counseling session and walked away. I believe God tried early on to protect us both from all the devastation and bitterness we endured.

I do believe Earl loved me the best way he knew how, but he didn't understand me like he thought he did ... like the mentors asked. As much as he felt ready for marriage, he wasn't ready to marry *me*. He was ineligible.

Mr. Iam Ready

"In the same way, you husbands must give honor to your wives. Treat your wife with understanding as you live together. She may be weaker than you are, but she is your equal partner in God's gift of new life. Treat her as you should so your prayers will not be hindered." (1 Peter 3:7, NLT)

Ineligible Bachelor #4:
Mr. Pho Bia

Tick, tick, tick. The hands on the clock moved.

Tick, tick, tick.

Ten more minutes until the end of the school year, I reminded myself. (Students are not the only ones who get excited for the end of the year.) I finished cleaning and organizing the bookshelves in my room while the students watched a movie. They had already had an end-of-the-year party during lunch.

Briiiiinnnng!

The school year was over! I had the students grab their backpacks and line up for dismissal. Like normal, I walked them to the dismissal gate to release them to their parents for the summer. A man I'd never seen before on campus walked up to me.

"Hey, I know you're happy right now!" he said, attempting to strike up a conversation. "I see that smile! Are you Ms. Laine?" he asked.

"Hi, yes and yes! Gosh, is it that obvious? And I am Ms. Laine," I confirmed.

Unqualified: The Ineligible Bachelor

He laughed at my response. "My name is Mr. Green. I subbed for you one day when you were absent. Your class was pretty good. I mean you had a couple of tough ones, but once they saw Mr. Green didn't play they fell in line."

"Yeah, I had a few!" I agreed. "They never mentioned you to me. What's your name again?"

"Mr. Green … Clark Green."

"Nice to meet you, Mr. Green." How ironic was it that his eyes were actually green?

"So, what are your plans for the summer?" he inquired.

"Oh, I plan on doing some traveling. I'm going to Las Vegas to my parents' house for a while and then to Boston to visit my friends," I shared excitedly.

I was in the beginning stages of my divorce and couldn't wait to go on vacation. Earl was still living in the apartment, but I was disconnected from him physically and emotionally. I knew at some point we needed to discuss "the next steps," which would ultimately be his moving into his own place.

It had been over a month since he received the divorce papers. Surely, he didn't think I was moving out of the apartment with my son. I hope he didn't think we were going to be roommates either. Even though it was awkward, it seemed like part of him felt content living the way we were.

Clark chimed in, "I normally wouldn't ask this, but since it is summer vacation, would you like to exchange numbers? Maybe we can have dinner or catch a movie over summer break?" I lived by a strict code to never mix my career life with my personal. I didn't even hang out with co-workers. I lived two separate lives—on purpose.

Mr. Pho Bia

I weighed it all out in my mind while he was still talking. Clark appeared to be laid-back. I thought, *it is over summer break. And dinner and a movie seem harmless. Why not.* We exchanged numbers and went our separate ways.

Clark called me that evening, and I had to walk out of the house to take his call. I didn't think he was going to call me that soon. We talked for about fifteen minutes getting to know each other. I learned he was born and raised in Los Angeles. I told him I was from Boston. His birthday was in January, and he was only a year older than I was. He learned my birthday was in September and celebrating my birthday was everything to me.

I told him I had a son in middle school who played tackle football. I discovered football and baseball were his favorite sports, and he even coached a high school team. I also learned that he had a two-year-old son. Clark went to Hampton University in Virginia, which was the same college I had wanted to attend, but instead I stayed in Massachusetts.

I thought that was so crazy because we would've been there at the same time. I wondered if we would have been friends in college or even dated. *Hmm, maybe, maybe not.* I wasn't one of those girls who was into the light-skinned, light-eyed brother movement in the '90s, so I may not have paid him any attention. Anyway, talking to him was like a breath of fresh air. He seemed like a nice guy, and he had a great sense of humor. I was glad we exchanged numbers.

A week after we met, and a few phone conversations later, we got together for dinner before I left for my travels. I arrived about ten minutes late and found him sitting outside on a bench. He looked a little annoyed.

Unqualified: The Ineligible Bachelor

I apologized for my tardiness; being on time is not one of my best qualities. I try, but even when I'm on time, somehow I still end up late. He accepted my apology and we walked into the restaurant.

We spent the next 90 minutes eating, talking, and laughing. After dinner, he invited me to a movie and I accepted. A white Lexus pulled up in front of my car so I could follow him to the theater. *Nice car,* I thought and smiled. After the movie, we agreed to hang out again when I came back from my vacation.

Chris and I started our vacation by driving to Vegas to spend time with family. From there, my sister, who worked for an airline company, and I decided to fly to Boston about a week later. Chris stayed in Las Vegas to hang out with his grandparents. My sister and I spent a few days with friends and then headed back to Las Vegas.

A day after I returned, Earl called to say he had moved out of the apartment while I was gone. He told me he took EVERYTHING with him. I was so infuriated because we had never had a conversation about who was keeping what.

My sister found me a flight back to Los Angeles early that afternoon. I wanted to get back quickly. I didn't want to waste time driving, and I didn't want Chris to be present during any drama. I called Clark and asked him if he could pick me up from the airport. I felt bad involving him in my drama, but he was eager to help.

I arrived at LAX the next afternoon and stood outside looking for Clark in his white Lexus. He came driving up in a black Acura that was at least ten years old. I barely recognized him in that car. *What the hell?* I was confused, but I didn't have the time or mental capacity to try to

Mr. Pho Bia

figure it out. I needed to get back to my apartment ASAP to see what Earl had taken.

When I got in the car, I saw his son in a car seat in the back. That was a surprise! It was not the best way to meet his child. In that moment, I felt slightly bamboozled.

I arrived at my apartment building and thanked Clark for giving me a ride. As I took the elevator up to the third floor, I was praying Earl hadn't wiped the apartment clean. If he had any decency, he would just take what was his before the marriage.

I took a deep breath and opened my apartment door. I walked in and gasped! The living room was empty and the walls bare. The sofa, chair, coffee table and end tables were gone. He had removed some artwork, but those were his before marriage. The dining room was untouched. The dining table was there as well as my 65-gallon saltwater fish tank; Tyson, Kahuna my trigger fish, and Neemo my clown fish were all there.

Next, I walked into Chris's room. *Whew!* Everything was intact. Then, I ran to my bedroom. My bed and television were there! I noticed some towels and sheets had been taken, but that was it. Basically, I needed to purchase a new living room set. I could kiss my upcoming trip to Italy with my sister goodbye. I had to take care of my home. I didn't want Chris coming back to a partially furnished home.

A couple of hours later, Clark called and asked if I wanted a fish dinner. He said he was going to pick it up and bring it over. It was sweet of him. What wasn't sweet? The empty living room I was standing in. Unfortunately, I had to come clean with Clark about my husband still living there during the divorce and how he had moved out and taken the living room furniture with him while I was away.

I accepted his offer for the fish dinner, and he and his son came over and we sat at the table eating and talking. His son was fascinated with the fish in my tank, just sitting there watching them while his dad and I talked. I explained my current situation to Clark, and he seemed very sympathetic. After we ate, Clark and his son went home.

Within a week, my living room was furnished. I was so proud of myself! It even looked better than the previous set. *Earl may have done me a favor!* I thought. Clark came over to see it and said it looked really nice. He didn't have anything to compare it to, but I appreciated the compliment anyway.

I got to know Clark a lot better that evening. He had been single for six months after breaking up with his son's mother. He shared that the relationship ended because he "wasn't ready to get married." Also, I learned he didn't believe in God. Hands down, that should've been a deal-breaker, but I was so angry with God because of the Earl catastrophe that I didn't care.

Mr. Pho Bia

I remember one particular day when I was in my room talking to God. I was yelling at him, *I did it your way! I was celibate and I trusted you! And look at the man you brought into my life! The so-called godly man. Your way didn't work. Now I'm going to do it my way!* I was so angry with God. So with Clark, I thought, *Well, he's an atheist, at least he's honest.*

I asked Clark at some point if he ever wanted to get married and have more children. Although I was going through a divorce, I wasn't closed off to remarriage, and I wanted another baby—one day. I was just checking his head space. My dream was to have a child with my new husband, who also would love and accept Chris as his own. We would be a complete family.

Clark said he wanted to get married in the future and would like to have another child as well. When he was responding, though, his eyes were as big as a deer's eyes in headlights. *Interesting,* I thought. But I didn't pay too much attention because we had just started hanging out. We weren't serious or exclusive.

Unqualified: The Ineligible Bachelor

One evening I was telling Clark I had put my son in football, and practice was starting soon. His eyes lit up and he got excited! (The exact opposite reaction to the getting married and having another baby conversation.) He shared memories of playing when he was my son's age. He seemed passionate about sports. We ended up watching a movie on TV and he went home. Eventually I needed to get back to Las Vegas and pick up Chris and my fur baby, Jojo.

Football practice was every night from mid-July to mid-August. My time was limited now so Clark and I started having more phone conversations. One day he asked if it would be okay to come to the park and watch Chris's football practice. I said it would be fine, and so I got to introduce my son to Clark.

Chris seemed to like him and appreciated his football knowledge and personal experience as a player and coach. I was such a sucker for anyone who expressed a genuine interest in my son. Chris was the key to my heart. My thoughts and feelings for Clark started to change. I started seeing him as more than a friend. He started coming to more practices and would even bring his son. Then he began coming to scrimmages and games. Clark was coming around a lot, and I was happy.

Sometime after having a conversation with Clark, my son decided to play football for his high school instead of the youth football team he was on. He left the team and played on his school's junior varsity team. Clark came to many of those games as well.

I spotted our family therapist at one of the games and introduced him to Clark. In the next session, the therapist told me to take things slow since I was going through a

Mr. Pho Bia

divorce. He thought I should take time to grieve the loss of Earl. He explained he was concerned that any triggers I had in my relationship with Earl would be projected onto Clark. Not only would that be unfair to Clark, but it also could pose unnecessary problems in the new relationship.

I disagreed because I felt no emotional connection to Earl (hindsight is 20/20). Needless to say, I did not take his advice and continued seeing Clark.

As September approached, I planned a bowling party for my birthday with some of my friends. I decided to invite Clark. This would be the first time he met any of my friends. A couple of days before the party, on my actual birthday, Clark picked me up at my house. I was so excited because he knew how important birthdays were to me—especially mine. I wondered what he had planned.

When he arrived, I noticed he wasn't dressed up, but I was. Okay, guess that rules out going somewhere special! It felt as if we were on two different pages. Then he stopped to get gas. *Hmm, that's strange,* I thought. *Why didn't he handle this beforehand?* When he got back into the car, I noticed he was kind of quiet and nervous. The energy felt weird. I started feeling uncomfortable as if a big letdown was coming, but I tried to play it off.

Sniffle, sniffle, I heard coming from Clark's direction.

Unqualified: The Ineligible Bachelor

Is he crying? I wondered. *Lomasi, keep your eyes forward,* I told myself.

Sniffle, sniffle, sniffle.

I looked over and tears were streaming down Clark's face. *What the?* I had never seen a man cry like this.

"Lomasi." *Sniffle, sniffle.* "I know it's your birthday and how important it is to you. I really wanted to do something special for you, but I just don't have the money. I had to pay some unexpected bills and my son's preschool tuition."

Sniffle, sniffle, sniffle. "I'm sorry for ruining your birthday. I did manage to get you a little something, but I wanted to do more," he sobbed.

I was speechless. I didn't know what to say because I'd never been in a situation like this. I felt sorry for him, but I was disappointed at the same time. I mean we met in June. If he had planned to be in my life as a friend or boyfriend, he had three months to plan something.

"Clark, it's okay," I consoled him. "I accept your apology. You're right, my birthday is everything to me, and who knew we'd still be talking. Just plan better for the next one."

He handed me a Bath & Body Works bag. I opened it in the car. The bag was filled with five small hand sanitizers. *Hold up! This is my birthday gift? Hand sanitizers? You could*

Mr. Pho Bia

have saved the $15 you spent on these, and we could have gone to IHOP. It's the thought that counts, right?

To his credit, I did always carry those hand sanitizers in my purse. He was observant. All I could say was "thank you." I couldn't wait to get home and hang my cute outfit right back up in the closet.

Over the next few months, Clark and I grew closer. I invited him to my parents' house in Las Vegas for Thanksgiving and he accepted. This would be the first time they all met. I allowed Chris to bring a friend as well. Clark offered to drive his sister's Lexus, the car he had driven when we first went out.

On the drive there, we had a flat tire. Clark was devastated. He got teary-eyed because it was his sister's car and she had entrusted him with it. I knew he didn't want to let her down. By this point, I was convinced Clark was a very emotional man. Don't get me wrong. I would've been pissed too, but I'm not sure I would have cried. He found a tire shop that was able to fix it, and we were back on the road in no time.

I introduced Clark to my parents, and we all hung out in the living room talking. Thanksgiving afternoon, we had an awesome meal and watched football. I had been learning a lot about football thanks to Clark. He taught me football terminology and plays at my son's games. Also, I had started watching it on TV with him and watched him play Madden. Surprisingly, I had an interest in playing Madden as well so Clark and my sister taught me.

Unqualified: The Ineligible Bachelor

While we were there, we took Chris and his friend to the "Strip," went to the malls, and went shopping for Black Friday deals. Before we headed back Saturday morning, I wanted to have a long conversation with my mom. I wanted to get her and my stepdad's opinion about Clark because I was starting to fall for him. My mom thought he was a nice guy but made a point of telling me he wasn't "the one." But to her, no one was ever the one!

Clark and I didn't celebrate Christmas together but exchanged gifts a few days before. We got each other a pair of True Religion jeans. Chris, Jojo, and I went to Las Vegas again to spend Christmas and New Year's with my parents. I guess Clark couldn't stand being apart because he drove out the night before New Year's Eve to spend it with me. We went to the "Strip" and partied with everyone else. We found a great location to sit and people-watch, drink, and have a good time.

Unfortunately, the Jack Daniels I'd been drinking earlier didn't mix well with the champagne I had for the countdown. My stomach didn't appreciate that combination, and I spent the wee hours of the morning throwing up. Clark was not attentive. He seemed a little freaked out to be around me. The "deer in headlights" look was back.

Mr. Pho Bia

In January, I decided to throw Clark a surprise birthday dinner. His family and friends would meet us at this nice restaurant near Beverly Hills. He even let me blindfold him and walk him into the restaurant. When we got to the table, he saw his friends and sister when I removed the blindfold and we all yelled, "Surprise!"

It was exciting to see him enjoying himself around his friends. I truly cared about Clark and wanted him to feel special. I also wanted him to see the way I celebrate birthdays for the special people in my life and model how I wanted to be treated for mine. Moving forward, he'd never have to wonder what he should do for mine. Just go all out!

Like most couples, we spent Valentine's Day together. We went to dinner and a movie and exchanged gifts. Our relationship continued to progress. My guard was down, and we fell in love. This felt different from the past couple of relationships. One reason was there was only a one-year age difference between us instead of the ten-year gap between me and all my previous boyfriends.

I started wondering about the possibilities of our future. Then I was jolted by an extremely disappointing event that occurred a couple of months later.

"Lomasi, you can't come to my son's birthday party. I don't feel comfortable bringing you to his grandmother's house."

"What?!" I yelled, as my body started to tremble. "What do you mean? I am around your son all the time."

"I don't want to make his mother uncomfortable and the party awkward," he said nervously.

Unqualified: The Ineligible Bachelor

"So, you can come to all of my son's events and to my parents' home, and I can't come to your son's birthday party?" I argued.

"This is why I didn't want to talk about his birthday party with you. I knew you'd want to go. It's my son's birthday, and I don't want any drama," he said coldly.

Drama? What did he really think of me? Why wasn't I worthy of being there? I had never experienced a rejection like that. I was hurt, sad, and confused all at once. *What is happening?!*

The day of the party, I was on edge the whole time. I was anxious. Part of me was hoping he would call and tell me he changed his mind and wanted me there. That moment never happened. My hurt went deeper, and my heart grew heavier with every hour that passed. I was getting sick to my stomach. *Why doesn't he want me there? Is he hiding something?* I tried to busy myself around the house. When the party was over, Clark finally called me. Although I was relieved, the pain persisted.

Summer was approaching and it would be a year since Clark and I met. The hurt of not being invited to the birthday party still lingered, but we remained together. I asked if he wanted to go away for our one-year anniversary. Clark disclosed that he was afraid of flying. He explained that he hadn't always been afraid, but after his son was born, the fear of dying set in.

Great. I loved traveling by air, land, and sea. I wasn't sure how this was going to work out in the future. We decided to go to Catalina Island. I dropped Jojo off at Earl's (an arrangement we made during our divorce) and took Chris to Las Vegas to stay with my parents.

Catalina was beautiful! The sky was bright, and the air was clean. Clark enjoyed getting in the ocean, but the water was too cold for me. We ate wonderful seafood while we were there and rented a golf cart to tour the island. Overall, we had a great time.

We arrived back at my apartment building late at night. I asked Clark to wait out front while I took my bags up to my unit and then I'd be back down. When I came back outside, Clark's car was gone. I called him immediately.

"Hey, why did you leave?" I asked, once I was back inside my apartment. "I was coming right back down."

"Why did I leave?!" he repeated, obviously irritated." I left because your crazy ass ex-husband walked up to me in my car acting like he had a gun!" he shouted.

"What?!" I asked in disbelief.

"Don't act like you didn't see him!"

Unqualified: The Ineligible Bachelor

"I didn't see him!" I insisted. "I went right into the building and got on the elevator."

"He walked over to my car as soon as you walked to the door," he explained. "That scared me, Lomasi. I saw my life flash before my eyes! I have a child! I'm not losing my life over a crazy, jealous ex-husband!" he shouted again. Clark was enraged.

All the joy we experienced in Catalina quickly evaporated. Unfortunately, this fiasco was not the last time Earl stalked Clark and me.

We managed to move past the stalking incidences, but Clark didn't trust me. He thought something was going on between Earl and me. Truthfully, there wasn't. But how do you convince someone who has been stalked twice by your ex-husband?

In the weeks that followed, we tried to get the relationship back on track. It would soon be going on 18 months. I wanted to see where Clark thought the relationship was headed. Some aspects of the relationship seemed better, but there were still some things left unresolved between us.

December was quickly approaching, and all the teachers were preparing a Christmas performance with their students. Clark's son was in preschool, and I knew he would be having a Christmas show. I asked Clark about it, and he confirmed there was a production. Days passed, and he never mentioned that performance.

I knew when it was and was waiting for him to tell me, but he didn't. I wanted to see how he was going to handle this after the birthday party ordeal. We were officially a year-and-a-half into our relationship, so I wondered what his excuse would be this time.

I asked him about it again a couple of weeks later, and he told me the show was that night. When I asked why he hadn't told me, he said he didn't feel comfortable inviting me to his son's school program. *Blah, blah, blah.* Same speech. Same song. This time I wasn't sad and heartbroken—I was livid! I wasn't going to keep playing this game. I was not going to be strung along by someone who didn't want a future with me.

After the performance, Clark and I had the tough conversation.

"Clark, we've been together for a year-and-a-half. This was yet another event of your son's to which you didn't feel 'comfortable' inviting me. It's very confusing to me, especially since you two are always at my house and attending my son's events. I'm starting to think it's not you that is uncomfortable, but his mother. Is that what it is?"

"No, his mother has nothing to do with this. She just got engaged to her boyfriend," he replied.

This was a great segue. "Clark, where do you see this going?" I asked. "Do you want a future with me?"

Unqualified: The Ineligible Bachelor

"Mmm ... ahh," he hemmed and hawed. "I can't see it right now, Lomasi," he admitted.

And there it was. The truth. His truth.

"I don't have my stuff together. I don't have a career. I'm a substitute teacher. I live with my sister. There's a lot I need to do for myself," he said, with tears in his eyes.

"I get it, Clark," I sympathized. "But why would you wait over a year to say this? I don't want to date for three years and you still not be ready." I stated my truth.

I decided to back down and give him a little more time and space from this conversation, but I would revisit it.

When I brought it up again, we were in my car parked at a gas station. I asked him the same question.

"Clark, where do you see this going?" I inquired again. "We are moving toward two years together in a couple of months. Do you see a future with me?"

"I like things the way they are, Lomasi," he replied. "Why mess it up? Can't we be like Oprah and Stedman?" he chuckled. He may have chuckled, but he was serious.

Did this man just say Oprah and Stedman? I asked myself. "No! We can't be like Oprah and Stedman!" I responded firmly. "I want to be remarried and have a family, Clark!"

Mr. Pho Bia

It was then and there it became crystal clear. A future with Clark wasn't going to happen. Ultimately, he feared commitment when it came to marriage. It wasn't me; it was him. He was unqualified to love me. He was right about one thing. He really needed to work on himself. *What if I had married him at that time? I would've married another ineligible man.* We had a good run with some major snags here and there, but fear got the best of him.

I chose to walk away. A future with Clark was not in my best interest. I can't lie; it was extremely hard ending it. It was my first time grieving a loss of a relationship. I met him when I was mad and disconnected from God; but the fact remained, Clark and I were unequally yoked.

I was still a believer and the daughter of the Most High. My Father wanted His best for me, his daughter. He already knew how that story was going to play out. Clark's rejection was God's protection.

About twelve years later, I ran into Clark at a Fourth of July festival in Los Angeles. As ginormous as L.A. is, he saw me from across a lot filled with food trucks. I had my head down eating my food when I heard someone call my name. I looked up to find Clark standing in front of me. I was

Unqualified: The Ineligible Bachelor

blown away. What are the chances? Hear me when I say that I hardly ever run into any one I have dated post break-up.

Nonetheless, he looked good. He had gained some weight but still looked the same. He caught me up on his life. The pros: He had truly worked on himself. He went back to college and earned a master's degree and settled into his career. His son was now in high school and an athlete. He had moved out of his sister's house. He even talked about some of his other relationships after us. The cons: He was four years shy of fifty and still not married.

I would have wasted so many years waiting for him to become "eligible." Although I was super proud of Clark and his accomplishments, the fact remained, he was never eligible. If I had known then what I know now, I wouldn't have endured so much disappointment and heartbreak.

"For I know the plans I have for you," says the Lord. They are plans for good and not for disaster, to give you a future and a hope." (Jeremiah 29:11, NLT)

"Don't team up with those who are unbelievers. How can righteousness be a partner with wickedness? How can light live with darkness?" (2 Corinthian 6:14, NLT)

Ineligible Bachelor #5:
Mr. Wido Wer

What are you looking for? Marriage. A committed relationship. Something Casual. Not sure.

I am looking for something casual, I thought, so I selected that option.

What's your name?

Lomasi Laine.

Upload a picture.

Oh, I need to find a cute one of me! I think I'll use this Miami picture. It shows me having a good time.

How tall are you?

I'm 5-foot 3¾ inches, but there was no fraction option so I chose 5 foot 4.

What's your ethnicity?

Black.

What's your religion?

Christian.

What's your job title? Highest degree?

I continued clicking away.

Unqualified: The Ineligible Bachelor

What are you looking for in a man? the next section asked. *What's your type?*

Hmm ... What IS my type? I began wondering. I never had a type per se. All the guys I had dated looked different, had different personalities, and different careers.

Age range? Without a doubt, this person had to be in my age range, so I chose 37 as the age limit.

Religion?

Christian.

Are you looking for matches 25 miles, 50 miles, or 100 miles away?

This wasn't my first rodeo. This was probably the third online dating site I had joined after divorcing Earl. Before I met Clark, I joined two sites. It was fun to go out and meet people, but there were no matches. Many of the men were surprised I looked like my picture. I had heard some horror stories from some of the guys.

When things started to develop with Clark, I terminated my memberships. But now, after six months of being single, I felt ready for companionship. I had everything else in place: career, finances, my mind, and emotions. I just wanted someone to talk to, go to dinner and a concert with, and maybe even travel together. Distance hadn't been a problem for me in the past, but this time I wanted to connect with someone closer, so I selected "25 miles."

I clicked "Done" and my search began for someone who looked and sounded interesting.

No. Click. *No.* Click. *No.* Click. *Interested!* Click.

I leaned back in my chair and thought for a minute. *Inhale ... exhale.* Then I shut down the computer and went to bed.

Mr. Wido Wer

The next day was New Year's Day. I woke up feeling optimistic, even though I slept through the countdown. My sister was visiting me for the holidays and I told her I had joined *Hot Chocolate,* an online dating site for black singles. I pulled up the website and showed her my profile.

I explained how it worked and showed her some of the people I was interested in and those who had shown an interest in me. I tried to convince her to set up an account and give it a try. She gave me a skeptical look and went back to watching her television show.

Ding. The chat notification went off and was flashing on my profile. *Hello,* it read.

Somebody wanted to chat with me. I checked out his profile before responding and realized he was one of the guys I tagged as being interested in. His profile read, *Age: 36; Profession: Sales; Religion: Christian; Height: 5'10; Children: 2; Enjoys: fine dining, music, and traveling.* His profile was impressive. *He literally enjoys the same things I do,* I marveled.

Here goes, I said to myself. I sent him a message and we continued a "get to know you" chat for the next 45 minutes. He seemed really cool; but heck, anyone can seem cool online. Then the next message appeared.

"Would you like to talk on the phone?"

Oh, wow! Do I want to talk with him on the phone this soon? I asked myself. I sat and weighed out everything I knew at the time. He did seem like a potential match. I had prayed for God to send me a companion. Maybe this is the one. *Girl, don't block your blessings,* I told myself while folding my hands in a prayer-like manner.

Unqualified: The Ineligible Bachelor

I asked the gentleman for his number because I didn't want to give him mine yet. He typed his number in the chat box and said his name was Mason; I told him my name as well. He asked if I was black. I laughed because no one ever thinks Lomasi is a "black girl's name." He was no exception.

I decided to take the plunge and give him a call.

"Hi, Mason? It's Lomasi ... from Hot Chocolate."

"Hi, Lomasi. How's it going?" he asked. "It's so cool to put a voice to the profile picture."

We continued getting to know each other, and he seemed just as cool on the phone as he had online. We had so much in common—from activities we enjoy, favorite television shows, favorite music artist, even the same favorite dessert from the same bakery. We even had similar conversations with God about sending a companion. It was the weirdest thing! To add a cherry on top, we were finishing one another's sentences! *Really? In the first conversation? What?!* I asked myself.

I have never had that many things in common with a man. And the chemistry was unbelievable. It was like we had known each other for years. It was kind of scary. Our first phone conversation lasted four hours! *I know, right!* We could have kept on talking, but he had to get up at 3 a.m. to go to work.

"Lomasi, would you like to go to dinner with me tomorrow?" he asked, before ending the phone call.

"Sure!" I responded. "Where would you like to meet?"

"You pick. It doesn't matter where. Don't worry about the price," he wooed. "Just tell me where you decide tomorrow, and I'll be there."

Mr. Wido Wer

"Okay! I will," I assured him.

"Okay, cool. I will call you tomorrow after work."

And just like that our first date was arranged. I was in disbelief. *Did this phone call really just happen? Is he too good to be true?* All kinds of thoughts and questions ran through my head, including the fact he was a widower. *Yes, you heard me.* A widower.

The next day I woke up thinking about what restaurant to choose. I had a few in mind that were located in Beverly Hills where I lived. I wanted to call my home girl, who always ate at fine dining restaurants, to get a second opinion. She named a few, and the last one she suggested was Mastro's, which is the one I selected.

She advised me to set up a reservation, which I did. Now I just needed to figure out what to wear. I also felt strongly about making a small gesture of appreciation to Mason for taking me to a fine dining restaurant not even twenty-four hours after talking on the phone.

I decided to get mini peach cobblers from the Cobbler Lady, which was our favorite dessert and bakery shop. *This is going to be such a sweet surprise.* I was so excited to meet him in person and prayed that he looked like his picture, and he wasn't crazy. Also, I prayed the vibe we had online and the phone would continue in person. *Lord, let this not be too good to be true*, I prayed out loud.

The next afternoon, I picked up the mini cobblers and went home to figure out what I should wear. I started rummaging through my closet looking for the most flattering outfit. I had lost a lot of weight due to a traumatic and stressful event in my life (I'll save that for another book), and I was still underweight. Many of my clothes just didn't fit properly.

It was so bad, a man once asked a friend of mine "if thin was in" after meeting for lunch. That hurt. I was working with a trainer on gaining healthy weight back. After I decided on an outfit that would best complement my body, my phone rang. "Mason-Hot Chocolate" displayed across my Blackberry screen.

"Hi, Lomasi. It's Mason. How's it going?"

"Hi! Good. Everything is going well!" I responded. "What about you?"

"I just got in from work. Were you able to decide on a restaurant?"

"Yes, I did!"

"What did you pick?

"Mastro's ..."

"In Beverly Hills?" he cut me off. "That is crazy! I was going to suggest Mastro's if you couldn't think of one. Wow, how is it that we think the same, have so much in common, and finish each other's sentences? It took ten years to reach that with my wife."

"I know, right? It is weird."

"So, what time do you want to meet?" he asked.

"It was suggested to make a reservation, so I made one for 9 p.m."

"Okay, cool. Let me get cleaned up and I'll meet you there. It should take me about an hour to get there depending on the traffic," he explained. "How long will it take you to get there?" I figured he was testing me because my profile said I lived in Beverly Hills.

Mr. Wido Wer

"I live close by, so it should take me about six minutes," I explained. "Just let me know when you get into the Beverly Hills area, and I will leave my house."

"Okay, cool. See you then."

I had a few hours to kill, so I spent time with my sister and son playing a card game.

I got ready then sat and waited. At 8:40 p.m. I started getting a little nervous because Mason had not called. He finally called about ten minutes later saying he had just gotten in the area and apologized for running a little behind. He had gotten lost trying to take back streets. I asked him to describe where he was and told him to stay there. I grabbed my coat and the cobbler and left to meet him. I found him a few minutes later and told him to follow me to the restaurant. We still made our 9 p.m. reservation.

We sized each other up outside the restaurant. He was nice looking, but definitely exaggerated his height on his profile—Mason was not 5'10! He looked about an inch taller than I am, and I was wearing medium-sized heels. That would put him at 5'7! He appeared rather skinny beneath his trendy clothing.

Mason and I got better acquainted as we enjoyed a wonderful meal. He shared that his friends called him Mase if I wanted to call him that too. He talked more openly about his children, especially his daughter. I learned that his aunt from Texas lived with him. She had helped with his wife when she was sick and currently helped him with his children.

We kept finding more things we had in common. We were both fans of German cars and had the same brands growing up. We were both germophobes. We both suffered from acid reflux disease. We both traveled to Miami with friends for our birthdays the same year. We both loved live music and concerts.

I decided I had the perfect place I wanted to take him after dinner if he agreed. At the end of our meal, I went to the restroom to make sure I didn't have anything in my teeth and reapply my lip gloss. I noticed Mason looked nervous when I headed back to the table. When I asked if everything was all right, he said he thought I was going to come back and end the date early.

"Actually, I was thinking since we both like live music, would you like to go listen to some at this place I love? It is not too far from here."

"Sure! What's the name of it?" he asked excitedly.

"Nic's Martini Grill and Bar. The live music is off the chain! My friend and I discovered it one night when she came to visit me," I explained. "It's almost 11:30 p.m.," I said, looking at my phone. "Do you want to head over there now?"

"Yeah, let's go!" Mason paid for the dinner, and we left.

The band was amazing that night. They were playing cover songs from the '80s. I handed Mason the bag containing the cobbler and he was surprised I was giving him a gift. I told him it was my way of showing thanks for the dinner invitation. He said it was very thoughtful and looked touched by the gesture. His mouth dropped when he opened the bag and pulled out the mini peach cobbler.

"Is this a peach cobbler from the Cobbler Lady?"

"You know it!" I said confidently.

Mr. Wido Wer

"Wow! I am blown away right now. Thank you so much, Lomasi. For real." He looked at me with adoration. "Are there spoons in the bag? Shoot, let's eat it now!" he said laughing.

We shared the peach cobbler, continued listening to the band and even dancing to a couple of songs. The time went by too fast. It was 1:30 a.m. and time to leave. Apparently, Mason didn't want the night to end because he asked if we could spend some more time talking. I told him I was fine with that.

We both pulled into a nearby drug store parking lot and Mason got into my car. He said he had some songs he wanted me to hear. He put in the first CD and the music began to play. I still couldn't believe we liked the same artist, Music Soulchild. We sat talking and listening to music for two hours like high school teenagers.

I started to get sleepy so Mason grabbed his CDs, and we thanked each other for an awesome night. He waved goodbye and smiled before he drove off. I knew he had at least a thirty-minute drive home—and it was now 3:30 a.m.—so I decided to call him and keep him company on his drive home. He thought that was sweet. Good thing I did because he got lost again leaving Beverly Hills. I stayed on the phone with him until he got close to his house and then we ended our night for real.

The next day was rather awkward. I didn't hear from Mason the whole day. Like most women, I thought about the wonderful date we had and how he felt about it. *Did he really like me? After all, we met online. He's probably had tons of online dates,* I thought. I tried to figure out why

Unqualified: The Ineligible Bachelor

he hadn't called or texted. I finally texted him late that afternoon, and he replied he was at the movies.

Mason and I talked several times over the course of the week. Each conversation was like our first one: engaging and endless. We could talk about anything, and before we knew it three or four hours had passed. We went on our second date in the second week. We really had good times together; it was effortless.

I noticed he started making comments about meeting his children. I didn't think much of it because it seemed too soon. By the third week, Mason asked me if I wanted to accompany him and his kids to Medieval Times. He said he wanted me to meet them. I asked if he thought it was too soon, but he assured me it wasn't. He also thought an outing was a good way for us to meet. I decided to go even though it was against my better judgment.

When Mason came to pick me up, he introduced me to his children. Tre was eight and rather quiet; Tammy was a spunky ten year old and talkative. They were adorable. We had a fun time until Mason kept insisting I take a picture with all three of them. I was already there against my better judgment, but I wasn't going to take a family photo and further confuse the children. It was early in our dating relationship, and I didn't even know how long it had been since Mason's wife had passed. I didn't even know if it was appropriate to ask.

Valentine's Day was quickly approaching, and Mason and I had agreed a week prior to date exclusively. His plan was to take me to an upscale Japanese restaurant in Hollywood Hills. I had suggested seeing *The Color Purple* on stage at the Pantages Theater. He told me he had never been to a professional stage play and agreed to go. Some friends of mine decided to join us for the play and it became a double date.

A couple days before the play, Mason bought me a dress; he was obviously into fashion and shopping, and I wasn't. That was the first time I had stepped into a mall in years. So far, this was one difference between us.

He picked me up for our Valentine's date and the restaurant was absolutely beautiful! We took lots of pictures and had another fabulous dining experience. Afterward, Mason and I met up with my friends outside the theater. I was completely impressed that Mason managed to get through the play without falling asleep; he had worked his regular twelve-hour shift that day. . After curtain call, we all left the theater and walked across the street to the W Hollywood and grabbed some cocktails.

Mason and I experienced our first disagreement on Mother's Day. He didn't acknowledge me on this special day. There was no card, phone conversation, or text wishing me a Happy Mother's Day. I felt rejected, and it really made me sad. He even came to visit me and didn't say a word.

Later that evening, I mentioned it to him, and he said it never crossed his mind because I wasn't his mother nor his children's. I explained I was still a mother, and a simple wish or gesture would have made me feel acknowledged. This was also the first time I noticed that Mason wasn't good at apologizing.

Not long after that, Mason and I decided to go to our first concert together. I really liked our chemistry; it was off the charts! We just got each other. I can't say I was in love, but I cared about him and enjoyed spending time with him. We saw each other every Tuesday and some Saturdays, but we talked on the phone every day. He and his children also attended church with me on Sundays.

We had recently been talking about traveling. He said he wanted to get into a habit of taking his family on a trip every year. I told him about the Disney Cruises that were supposed to be an awesome experience for children and adults. He thought it was a great idea and said he was going to research it. During a phone call a few days later, he said he was ready to book the trip and invited Chris and me to join them.

Initially, I was hesitant because I didn't want to impose on their family vacation. Once he reassured me he really wanted me to go, I wondered how my son—who was now seventeen—would feel hanging out with an eight year old, an eleven year old, and two adults. *It would make an awesome graduation gift though,* I reasoned. Chris would be graduating from high school in a few weeks.

After much consideration and Mason's persuasion, I agreed to go. But I asked him if we could surprise my son at his graduation luncheon I had planned. I really was swept off my feet with this gracious gesture by Mason. I said it before, "my son is the key to my heart." Mason just unlocked it.

Graduation Day arrived! My mom flew into town to witness her only grandson walk across the stage and receive his diploma. My dearest friend, who had known my son since he was eight, came to show her love and support. Mason and his kids arrived late and eventually joined us at our seats. It was such a joyous and proud moment for me as a mom. Hearing my son's name being called brought tears to my eyes.

The teenage years were no walk in the park and for my son to see this moment meant more than words could express. As parents, we want to see our kids win at this game called life. As a single mom, a black single mom at that, the odds are stacked against you along with every stereotype out there for young black men.

When we finally heard Chris's name, we went crazy and applauded and whistled celebrating him. After the ceremony, we took pictures and then headed to lunch. Everyone shared nice memories about my son and presented him with gifts. That was when Mason gave him the itinerary of the cruise and the plane ticket to Orlando. Chris was overcome with emotion by all the love expressed for him that day.

Unqualified: The Ineligible Bachelor

Before long, we were on our way to Orlando. We decided to go a day early so we could visit Disney World before our five-day cruise to the Bahamas and Disney's private island Cast Away Cay. It was so awesome to see everyone's face the day we boarded the ship. Except for me, it was everyone's first time to cruise, and they didn't know what to expect.

The Disney Cruise was nothing short of amazing. The food was delicious and they had entertainment for every age group. Tre and Tammy got to meet kids from different states and countries that they kept in touch with via social media. Chris had no problem finding other teenagers to hang out with, and Mason and I took advantage of some of the adults-only activities. It was probably one of the best experiences I ever had.

My feelings for Mason were growing, and I needed to ask God about my purpose in Mason and his children's lives. I didn't want to waste his time or be another loss for Tre and Tammy. This was the first time since Earl that I turned to God about a relationship. The demise of my marriage to Earl was why I stopped seeking him.

Full of anger and bitterness, I didn't seek him when I dated Clark. After that downward spiral, I reconnected to God realizing his way was best after all. No matter what, he gives us free will to do what we want. Regardless of being at church every Sunday and Bible study every Wednesday, I learned Earl was responsible for his behavior and how he treated me, not God.

It took hitting rock bottom after dating Clark for God to get my attention again. I decided to seek God through prayer and fasting. It was in my prayer time that God led me to Genesis 2:18, "Then the Lord God said, it is not good for the man to be alone. I will make a helper who is just right for him" (NLT). *God, am I to be Mason's help meet?* I asked. *Is this why we have this deep, unexplainable connection to each other? Am I to be his wife?*

I sat in silence meditating on the verse and pondering on this revelation. *Then that settles it,* I told myself. I didn't know the how or the when, but Mase and I were going to be married.

Two days passed and I hadn't heard from Mason. When I called to check on him, he didn't sound like himself. He sounded sad and distant. In that moment, something told me to ask him about a topic I had not mentioned since meeting him.

"Mason, may I ask you something?"

"Sure," he said.

"We never talked about this, but, umm ... when did your wife pass away?"

"Wow, what made you ask that?"

"Well, you seem down and distant. I have seen this before in people who lost a loved one. I have seen it with my son with the loss of his grandfather, and I have experienced the same feeling," I explained.

"Actually, she passed away today, last year. Today makes a full year," he said. He then started to explain what happened the week before her death, and I could hear his pain and sadness. Mason was grieving.

I didn't know how he masked it so well. That meant when we met, she had been dead only four months. It was apparent; Mason hadn't been dealing with his grief. I gave him my support and tried to console him.

Unqualified: The Ineligible Bachelor

I must admit, I didn't know what to do with this new information. It threw me off, especially after riding on the glory cloud from God saying we were to be married. *But how, God? This man is grieving the loss of his wife.* It was like the blissful lenses I had been wearing were removed. From that moment, I started to see all the things I didn't see before ... one by one.

I decided to continue to date Mason by faith. I was trusting what God told me. About two months later, we decided to take our first trip alone as a couple. I picked San Francisco as a weekend getaway. It was usually chilly in November, but San Francisco was experiencing a heat wave. The weather was perfect! We ate at nice restaurants, took a bus tour of historical and monumental places, and took pictures at the Golden Gate Bridge. It was one of the most memorable trips we took together.

The most wonderful time of the year, and my favorite holiday, was fast approaching. Mason asked me what I wanted for Christmas. I told him I wanted some UGG boots. Anyone who knows me knows I love boots. I described the boots to him and sent him the website. I asked Mason what he wanted. He said he didn't want anything, but I had already picked out the perfect gift for him. I was going to buy him a new iPod. I knew he would love and appreciate this gift.

Mr. Wido Wer

My sister flew in for the holidays. On Christmas Eve, Mason and his kids joined my sister, Chris, and me for a Christmas Eve church service. Afterward, Mason and the kids decided to sleep over since we were all hanging out at my house. I noticed he didn't bring any gifts over for his children. *Maybe they're in the car,* I thought, *or maybe they're at his house. But why would he want to stay over here? Doesn't he want the kids to be home to open their gifts?*

When I asked him about it, he told me he was having a problem with their behavior in school and at home. I found it a bit strange, but I understood his decision was based on their behavior. My sister, Chris, and I had gifts for each other, so I was a little apprehensive about how his kids would feel Christmas morning.

My son and sister woke up first and then me. We started passing out our gifts to each other and opening them. It was a bit awkward as Mason and his kids watched us. After we opened our gifts, I passed out gifts to Tammy, Tre, and finally Mason. The kids were so happy. Mason was beyond excited when he opened his iPod.

I was surprised his kids didn't look devastated since their dad hadn't given them any presents. They probably thought what I initially thought, *they must be at home.* Then it hit me. *Wait a minute ... he doesn't have a gift for Chris and me either.*

I also surprised my son with a birthday cake since his birthday was a few days before Christmas. I had already given him a card with money so he could go shopping. While we were singing "Happy Birthday," I saw a side of Tre I hadn't seen before. He sat with the meanest scowl on his face and refused to sing.

When asked why he wasn't singing, he yelled that he didn't want to. My sister and I simultaneously told him to excuse himself from the group and sit somewhere else if he didn't want to celebrate. Mason and the kids left shortly after we ate the ice cream cake. And still I had no gift and no explanation.

I never did get one either. A few days later, I was visiting Mason's aunt who said she wanted me to stop by to pick up Christmas gifts for Chris and me. She said she couldn't believe Mason had not gotten the kids anything for Christmas. Then she asked me what he got me for Christmas. I told her I didn't receive anything either. Her mouth dropped open; she was flabbergasted.

During my visit, I found out Mason had bought his aunt a pair of UGGs. I was furious and disappointed ... again. It looked like Mason and I needed to have a conversation about this. But how?

"Mason, I understand why you chose not to get the kids gifts for Christmas. But I've been racking my brain trying to figure out why you didn't get Chris and me one—especially after we asked each other what we wanted."

"I wasn't in a good place financially to get you a gift," he responded.

Lie! I screamed in my head.

Mr. Wido Wer

"I had so many things come up that I needed to pay. But, I told you I didn't want anything."

"Damn, you couldn't get a card … some flowers … some lottery scratchers at least?" I asked disgustedly. "Mason, it hurt my feelings to know you didn't get me anything and didn't try to solve the problem another way. You just chose to get me nothing."

"I'm sorry that you feel this way." His apology sounded pathetic.

"You're sorry I feel this way?" I asked sarcastically. "You're not sorry for not getting me a gift after implying you were? Honestly, I feel you didn't get me or Chris anything because you didn't get the kids anything. It's like you didn't want them seeing you do something for us since they didn't receive anything from you. Their behavior got them in this boat and that has nothing to do with me. And that is so messed up!"

"No, that is not the case, Lomasi. You are a grown woman. The kids' consequences don't have an impact on what I do for you," he said, trying to reassure me.

"Then how did you manage to go to Bloomingdales and pick out UGG boots for your aunt and not think of me—knowing that's what I told you I wanted when you asked me?" He was not winning this one. Nothing he could say was going to fix the problem. I remained disappointed.

New Year's Eve and our one-year anniversary were quickly approaching. I asked Mason if he wanted to go to a New Year's Eve party. At first, he didn't seem interested and didn't know how to communicate that to me. I noticed Mason retreating again. I was starting to see a pattern. When he was worried about hurting my feelings, he would retreat, not talk to me about it, and take whatever discomfort came with it.

Well, I wasn't going to let him off that easy. I brought it up again and mentioned it was our first New Year's together. I told him it was special and held a lot of memories because we met on New Year's Day. We wound up spending time with the kids and then going to a party where we had a fabulous time.

Around March we took our second couple's vacation to Miami. The few days there were romantic and amazing. It was on a patio near the beach where our first conversation about "growing old together" took place. I knew God told me I was to be his wife, so it didn't come as a huge shock, but I was still surprised he was talking about it. He sounded very sincere. My feelings grew even deeper for Mason after that conversation.

Unfortunately, a few months after our trip to Miami, I learned my school district was doing a mass layoff, and as of June 30 I would be unemployed. I was praying they would hire me back before August. I had a little over a month to come up with a plan B and a plan C.

Mr. Wido Wer

It was toward the end of June I noticed Mason exhibiting some peculiar behaviors. I couldn't put my finger on it, especially when he surprised Chris and me with a trip to Hawaii with him and his kids. Like always, the vacation was fascinating, and we all had a great time.

It is said, when one door closes another one opens, right? In that season of my life, it seemed every door closed at once and nothing opened. I wasn't going to be rehired as a teacher in my district. I'd been collecting unemployment over the summer, but it wasn't enough to cover my rent and bills. Fear and panic started to set in. As a single mom, I'd always been able to provide for my son and keep a roof over his head.

I prayed so much during this time, but it was as if God's hands were over his ears. Thank God for my landlord who sympathized with me and allowed me to pay my rent late. I started to brainstorm the possibilities of moving back East or to Seattle with my uncle and aunt. I didn't want to move back home, so I began looking at school systems in the Seattle area.

Simultaneously, I continued applying for jobs in southern California. I broke the news of possibly relocating to my son who was attending junior college. Meanwhile, Mason was back to his reclusive ways. I just couldn't

Unqualified: The Ineligible Bachelor

understand it. While I was going through this hardship, he offered no emotional support and instead seemed to pull away.

September arrived and things looked hopeless; I still hadn't locked down a job.

My birthday, the one positive I had to look forward to, was approaching. Mason wasn't answering my calls. I remembered it was the same time last year that he displayed this same behavior—the first-year anniversary of his wife's death. Now this was the second-year anniversary.

I decided to drive out to his house to check on him and make sure he was okay. He was surprised to see me when he answered the door. I had expected him to be sitting quietly, depressed and grieving. No. He was watching ESPN and eating peanuts. *Is he serious?* I thought to myself as my blood began to boil.

"Hey, what's up, Lomasi," Mason said nonchalantly. "What brings you out here?"

"Umm, you! You have not answered my calls in three days. We went through this last year around this time, so I came out here to check on you. What's going on? Are you okay?" I asked, trying to remain calm.

"I've been having a rough week. People have been saying I need to take some time," he explained. "I'm damaged goods, Lomasi. I'm having a tough time with the loss of my wife. I know I'm going to probably regret saying this, but I don't think I'm the man for you. There is someone out there who will love and appreciate you and who can make you happy."

An icy chill went through my body, and I started trembling. *Did he just break up with me? Three days before my birthday? What the hell is he talking about?* Thoughts began to fire off in my head. *Who are "people"? What do they know about our relationship? Why is he listening to "people"? We both had agreed that this was something unique and amazing that we had never experienced before. We truly felt it was an act of God.* Question after question popped up, and the more confused and disgusted I became. The trembling grew worse.

"Lomasi, say something," he pleaded.

"What is there to say? I thought we were on the same page. You and "people" have decided. And happy birthday to me!" I shouted walking to the door.

Mason reached for my arm to stop me. "Lomasi, wait. I need to figure this out."

I pulled my arm back. "Don't touch me," I said, gritting my teeth and walked out the door. I refused to look back and walked directly to my car. When I drove off, I looked in the rearview mirror and Mason was standing in front of his house with his hands on his head. He knew what he was letting go. Just like that, door number two slammed in my face.

Jobless, boyfriend-less, and hopeless were my new reality, and I was terrified. *God, you told me I am to be his wife. How come you took him away?* I cried out. I wasn't mad at God. I was like a child questioning a parent after being promised something that didn't happen. I didn't understand why this was happening ... what God was doing.

What I felt so sure about was now ripped out of my life. This was when I first learned the concept of pruning. "God is pruning you," people would say. I ran so quickly into my Father's arms because, at that point, I had nowhere else to turn. The more I pressed, his answer remained the same: "Wait on the Lord."

Over the next few weeks, Mason occasionally sent little text messages. I guess they were "feelers" to test the water since breaking things off. I kept my responses short. One evening his aunt called and asked if he was at my house because she had Tammy and Tre. Mason was supposed to pick them up after work, but he never showed up. The kids wanted to go home, but Mason wasn't answering their calls or hers. I told her he wasn't with me.

I started to get worried and told her I would try calling him; I got no answer. A nervous feeling settled in my stomach. I called his aunt back and told her I would go check on him. I drove to his house at 10 p.m. His car was in the driveway, but there were no lights on in the house.

Mr. Wido Wer

I called his aunt back and she was really worried. I told her I could go in, but I would need her keys since I had given mine back to Mason when he broke up with me. I drove to her house, got her keys, drove back to Mason's house, and let myself in. The house was pitch black. There was no sign of Mason. I climbed the stairs to the bedroom praying I wouldn't find his lifeless body.

As I approached the room, I could hear his fan running. *Oh, he must be asleep. Maybe he had a rough day at work and came home, ate, and passed out*, I thought. I opened the bedroom door and turned on the light. There was Mason lying in bed asleep with another woman. An icy chill went through my body.

"Mason!" I shouted, shaking his arm.

He woke up and saw me standing over him.

"Lomasi! What are you doing here?!" He sat straight up like he had seen ghost. When he sat up, the woman next to him woke up.

It took every bit of self-control I could muster to keep from lunging forward and snatching that woman out of bed and beating them both.

"How did you get in my house?" he demanded.

"I thought you had to figure things out because "people" were telling you to take your time," I mimicked.

Unqualified: The Ineligible Bachelor

"And you're here in bed with another woman?! Your kids have been looking for their dad and you have been ignoring them. Your aunt has been calling you and is worried sick. She called me panicking and I got worried." By this time my blood was boiling.

"But there was nothing wrong with you. There was NEVER anything wrong with you. You seem to be doing just fine! This is the closure I needed!" I shouted and stormed out the bedroom.

"Lomasi, you handed your keys back to me. How did you get in here?!" he asked, following me.

"Don't worry about it!" I snapped and continued to make my way downstairs.

"You need to leave my house! This is an invasion of my privacy," he snarled, as he followed me to the front door.

"You don't ever have to worry about me coming here again. I am done with you, you liar!" I said with the silver tongue my family said I had.

"Lomasi, how did you get into my house?" he asked again before I walked out the door. "Did you have another key made before you gave me mine back?"

"Don't worry about it," I said, gritting my teeth. I refused to give him a satisfactory answer. I walked out the door and didn't look back.

I was infuriated, numb, devastated, and more confused than ever. More questions raced through my head as I drove to his aunt's house to return her keys. Her giving me those keys was a secret that was never going to be disclosed. But they not only unlocked the door to Mason's house, they also unlocked a door to truth and exposed a two-timing traitor.

Mr. Wido Wer

Over the next week, Mason called several times to talk about what happened. He even had the audacity to ask me why I left in such a hurry that evening! This fool said he wanted me to "fight for him" for a lack of better words. Not fistfight, but in his words, "stand my ground" and claim my man.

He compared it to a situation his first wife encountered with him and another woman while they were dating. He explained that he and the other woman were hanging out but his first wife refused to leave. He said the other woman left, therefore putting his ex-wife in the "winner's circle" because she claimed her man. He went on about how he felt that solidified her feelings for him because she knew what she wanted and didn't back down. For him, it put into perspective where things stood between them.

I told him I wasn't 'that girl' and I don't and won't play games. He then started to digress, saying he was damaged goods and a curse. Somehow, he managed to manipulate the narrative and become the victim during my heartbreak and devastation. (This would become a horrible pattern down the line.)

As the job search remained hopeless and there were no prospects of being hired for a teaching job anytime soon, I decided to downsize my living conditions. I made plans

Unqualified: The Ineligible Bachelor

to move into a one-bedroom apartment. It was perfect timing because Chris had found a college he wanted to attend that came with student housing. As long as he had a roof over his head, I was content.

I also decided after December 30, if I had not spoken to Mason, then I would just write him off. I refused go into the new year with his wishy-washy ways. I prayed to God that day asking that His will to be done. On December 31, Mason called asking me to go to dinner for New Year's. I took that as God's will and accepted Mason's invitation.

That next year, things were surprisingly better between us. Our relationship was slowly getting back to normal—even though I was still haunted by memories of "that night." Mason decided to go to counseling to deal with his grief, single parenthood, as well as other stuff, but he only attended a few sessions.

I started working at a university and took on a summer job working with gifted children. That summer, we took the kids to Las Vegas instead of taking a big trip. By the end of the summer, I was hired back by my school district.

My birthday was approaching, and I was nervous remembering how the last one ended in heartbreak and devastation. But Mason took me to dinner, and it was a pleasant birthday. His 40th birthday was coming up, and I convinced him to have a little shindig with a few of his friends at our favorite martini place. I decorated with "40" décor, candles, bling, and mini desserts. Mason was genuinely touched and it turned out to be a great night.

That Christmas, my mom visited me. Chris, his girlfriend, mom, and I went to church on Christmas Eve; Mason, Tammy, and Tre joined us. Early on Christmas

Mr. Wido Wer

Day, my mom and I cooked a spread of food and took it over to Mason's house for Christmas dinner. Being all together was such an enjoyable time as a family. I started thinking back to what God had said, "you are to be a help meet," and the thoughts of marriage resurfaced.

As the New Year rang in, Mason and I were entering our third year together. It was now time to really look at where things were headed. The sting of "that night" was finally beginning to fade.

Then one night, I had a dream about us getting married. The décor was in place at a wedding venue, and the groom and wedding guests had on formal attire. Mason got on the microphone and started pouring his heart out to the guests. He talked about not being ready to get married.

When I woke up, I knew God was talking to me (as he usually does through dreams). *Mason wasn't ready,* I repeated to myself. I didn't tell Mason about the dream, and I didn't put any pressure on him. I just continued to commit everything to prayer and leave it in God's hands. *Lord, I don't know how and when ... I just know what you said. Help Mason with whatever he's going through, and help me to be patient,* I prayed.

A few months after that dream, and out of nowhere, Mason told me he wasn't ready to get married. He explained he was still grieving, but there was someone out there who could make me happy and would want to marry me. *Not this sh*t again!* I screamed in my head. Once again, Mason threw a dagger to my heart. *Lord, I can't take any more of the heartache and wishy-washy behavior. Maybe I didn't hear you correctly,* I began second guessing.

Unqualified: The Ineligible Bachelor

At that moment, I chose to separate myself from Mason and not look back until God said something different. Mason was ineligible to love me because his heart wasn't whole. As much as I tried to keep him from saying he was damaged goods, the truth is ... he was. The record kept skipping at the same part of the song.

As beautiful as our chemistry felt and as strong as our connection was, neither could mend the ginormous holes in Mason's heart. He needed God to fill every hole so he could be whole again and love me with a whole heart. And until that happened, he would continue to be ineligible—and I would continue being tossed between the land of happiness and the sea of despair.

"Wait on the Lord; be of good courage, And He shall strengthen your heart; Wait, I say, on the Lord!" (Psalm 27:14, NKJV)

"But those who wait on the Lord shall renew their strength; they shall mount up with wings like eagles, they shall run and not be weary, they shall walk and not faint." (Isaiah 40:31, NKJV)

Ineligible Bachelor #6:
Mr. Dawaitis Over

Several weeks passed and I had little contact with Mason. I did have one short conversation with him about a stranger who came up to him in a store and started telling him about God and gave him his devotional book. Mason felt that moment was God ordained and it really touched his heart. I guess he felt compelled to share it with me.

That was the only call I accepted from Mason in the course of three weeks. It was hard not to answer calls and respond to text messages. After all, I was used to speaking to him several times a day.

On Memorial Day, just about the fourth week of no contact, Mason texted me that he was going to a barbecue at a mutual friend's for the holiday. While he was telling me this, I was preparing a fruit salad and dip to bring to the same party. *How ironic,* I thought while rolling my eyes.

I was a little nervous because I wasn't sure if it was "time" to see him (meaning God's timing). I couldn't back out after committing to bring an item for the potluck. I tried to figure out how Mason knew about the barbecue because his name or email wasn't on the Evite. Clearly, I didn't tell him about it because I was keeping my distance.

Many of the couples Mason and I had attended Life Group with during the past year were at the party. I didn't see Mason anywhere. *Whew! Maybe he was just bluffing or trying to test me,* I thought, relieved. I saw the hostess of the party and went over to speak with her. She was aware of what I was going through with Mason.

I asked if she had invited him. She apologized and said yes, because he called her asking if she and her husband were hosting a Memorial Day event. *Hmmm, he called her to inquire ... interesting.* He insinuated that she had invited him. I told her not to worry about it because he hadn't shown up.

I brought the fruit salad and dip to a table in the dining area that had a large spread of food. I decided I wanted to eat as well. I walked to grab a paper plate. There stood Mason, piling his plate with corn tortilla chips. My heart started racing. He didn't look like himself. He was all scruffy and his hair wasn't combed. In fact, he looked like he had just rolled out of bed.

It was so awkward with just the two of us standing at the table; he was at one end and I was at the other. I could've easily walked back out, but then he looked up at me.

"Hi, Lomasi. How's it going?" he said coolly. "Wow, there's so much food! What's good to eat here?"

"Oh. Hi, Mason," I replied, acting like I hadn't seen him. *Did I really just say, Oh, hi?* I started walking past the table toward the kitchen.

Mr. Dawaitis Over

"Umm, I don't know. I haven't eaten anything yet," I replied.

"Did you bring anything?" he asked.

"I did. I brought the fruit salad and dip," I said, pointing to a tray on the other side of the table.

"Oh, cool. I will get some of that."

I walked over to the table and grabbed a plate when he was done. But he sat down in a chair near the table instead of leaving. I tried to ignore him as I put food on my plate.

"Lomasi, can I talk to you please?" he asked, walking over to me. "There is so much I want to talk to you about."

"No. I don't have anything to say to you, Mason."

"I've had a lot of time to think. I miss you so much," he confessed. "I have so much I want to say."

I had to stay strong because at the end of the day, I knew he was ineligible to love me. The last thing I needed was to get sucked back into that cycle that kept leading me to rejection and pain.

"Can I just have five minutes of your time then? I can talk while you eat your food," he offered. "Please?"

"You have five minutes, Mason."

He started telling me about his encounters with God over the past few weeks. Unexpected encounters that happened in phone conversations, stores, church, and parking lots with people he knew or complete strangers. He shared how God had been talking to him about himself and his actions, his children, and me, among other things. He apologized for his behavior and not treating me the way I deserved.

"I accept your apology and I forgive you," I said sincerely. "That means a lot to me, honestly." I stood up to go outside because, bottom line, I knew he wasn't ready for the next stages of our relationship. And I didn't want to keep going round and round with him. Even though he had encounters with God, he made no mention about the future. He was still ineligible.

"Wait, where are you going?" he asked, looking confused.

"You asked for five minutes. I listened and accepted your apology. I am happy God spoke to you so many times during these past few weeks. Now I'm going to head outside to hang out."

"Wait! I have more to say, but I know I only had five minutes." he said. "Can we leave and go somewhere so I can finish?"

"Leave and go where?" I asked, just a little apprehensive.

"Let's go to a restaurant."

"A restaurant? We are at a barbecue! How does that make sense?" I asked.

"I am starving. This food was more for snacking and wasn't filling. Will you meet me, please? We don't have to stay any more than thirty minutes—after I get my food," he clarified.

Thirty minutes, huh? Yeah, we'll see.

"Mason, you have thirty minutes and then I'm getting on the road and going home," I said firmly.

I said my goodbyes to my friends and walked out to my car. Mason came out a few minutes after me and got into his car. I followed him to El Toritos, but to his surprise, it was closed.

"Wait, Lomasi. Can we please find another place to go? I didn't know they would be closed."

Mr. Dawaitis Over

"It's a holiday," I chimed. "Where now, Mason?" I asked impatiently. "Can't you just say what you need to say now? You are right here and have my attention." I pointed out.

At this point I was ready to get in my car and go home.

"No, I can't tell you right here. Not like this." He said unhappily.

"OK, where?" I asked.

"Let's try TGIF's. It's just ten minutes from here." He suggested.

"Thirty minutes, Mason!" I reminded him.

When we got to the restaurant, Mason ordered an appetizer, chicken breast meal, and a cocktail! I started to get annoyed right away since this was supposed to be a thirty-minute conversation. Then he started making small talk and I grew even more annoyed. *I know he didn't make a big production for small talk,* I said to myself.

"Sooo ..." I cut in, wanting him to get to the point. "What else did you want to talk about?"

"Geesh, girl! Patience," he joked. "I'm going to get to it."

It was hard to be in a joking mood with him when I shouldn't have been there in the first place. Now with all the "fluff," I was getting mad at myself for agreeing to go. He finally began talking once the waiter brought his food.

"Lomasi, God has been speaking to me during these past weeks. As you know, he talks to me by using other people to deliver a message. I've had so many of these encounters," he reiterated. "Again, I apologize for my behavior and not treating you the way you deserved. I've had a lot of time to think. I don't like us apart. I have been miserable over the past few weeks. I love you so much. I'm a better man with you in my life. You do it for me, girl," he confessed.

"Our chemistry and connection are like no other. I didn't have this chemistry with my wife like I do with you. That's why I know what we have is special. I don't want to lose that. I really want to grow old with you. I want to get married!" Mason announced, looking directly into my eyes.

And there it was. Those words I'd been praying to hear. *I want to get married*. Now, I didn't know what to think: be happy or be leery. Was this God's timing?

"Wow, I am speechless, Mason," I responded.

"Lomasi, remember talking about growing old together when we were in Miami? I just want to be happy. I want us to be married." he restated. "What about you? Do you still want to grow old with me?"

"Of course, I do, Mason. I just don't know if it's the right time. I mean, have you honestly had enough time to really grieve the loss of your wife?"

"Yes!" Mason affirmed. "I told you I had a lot of time to think, reflect, and release. I spent some time talking to her and closing that book. I am ready!"

His excitement started to become contagious, and I started to laugh.

"I don't want to wait anymore. I want to get married this year!" he said adamantly.

Okay, it was the end of May and he said, "this year." That meant planning a wedding in about five to six months. I had heard of people doing it in less time, so it wasn't a far-fetched idea. My mind drifted and I began imagining. *A winter wedding—or better yet, a wedding on our anniversary in January. That's close to the end of the year. Oh, that would be really special,* I thought.

"This year could work," I said quickly coming out of the clouds and approving his idea.

"When's your next school vacation?"

"Mid-June until mid-August. The next one after that is in November during Thanksgiving and then Christmas break of course."

"My next vacation is in July," Mason added. "I have two weeks. Lomasi, let's get married in July!"

"In July!?" I yelled. "Mason, you do know my family is on the East Coast, right?"

"Yeah, but I don't want to wait, Lomasi. We can do it!"

I went back into the clouds. *Hmm … July? July 4th weekend? Ugh! That will be too expensive for people to fly out to Los Angeles. Oh, wait. What about my dad's birthday, July 13? Now, that would be special.*

We both pulled out our phones and began looking at the calendar. My dad's birthday fell on a Saturday, and I knew that Saturday was an expensive day to have a wedding. We considered the possibility of a Sunday wedding. We finally chose July 7 as our wedding date. July, the seventh month, was my dad's birth month, seven was the number of his mother's birthday, and seven is the number of completion. We had thirty-nine days to plan a wedding!

When I got home that evening, I was still speechless. Then I went straight into analyzing mode. All kinds of thoughts engulfed my mind. *Was he REALLY ready or would he flip-flop? Was it truly God's timing? Was that a real proposal or was he testing me? And where's the ring? How would the transition work with me moving in with him, Tammy, and Tre?* I didn't have any peace and I surely didn't have any answers, so I did what I knew to do: pray.

A couple days later, God confirmed to me through his word that it was time. I had a sense of peace. I hoped Mason was going to do this correctly—offer me a legitimate proposal with a ring. That weekend, Mason and I had a late lunch date. Afterward, he pulled into a diamond ring store because he wanted me to try on rings. I couldn't believe it! Everything seemed to be falling into place.

It was so much fun walking around the display cases, but it also was overwhelming. Mason tried to help, but the rings he picked out weren't flattering on my small hands. Finally, a woman came over to help us and we selected an engagement ring and wedding band that we both liked. I didn't leave there with the diamond ring because it had to be sized, so I had to trust that Mason wouldn't change his mind about buying it. That was hard since he was known to flip-flop.

Mason and I started discussing locations and decided on a vineyard-style wedding. We found the perfect winery in Temecula, California. Two weeks after our conversation at the restaurant, and twenty-four days before our wedding, there was still no proposal and no ring. He had not mentioned either in our conversations. I tried not to worry and focused on researching various wedding vendors near the winery.

A week later, my matron of honor and I went looking for her dress. I had already purchased my wedding dress. It was stressful since it was considered short notice in the

Mr. Dawaitis Over

bridal world. Somehow, I managed to pull a muscle in my back and had to call it quits for the day. I decided to stay at Mason's house because it hurt to sit and drive.

The next morning, I was still in pain and couldn't get out of bed. Mason headed out to grab us some takeout breakfast. About forty minutes later, he walked into the bedroom with the bag of food. As he began handing me my food, he said the restaurant didn't have a particular item in my order. I was so disappointed because I was starving.

He proceeded to show me what he got instead. Out of nowhere, he presented me with the diamond ring! Right there in the bed, in my pajamas, with a sore back, and a funky attitude over missing breakfast items—Mason formally proposed to me. I was embarrassed, but after hearing Mason's sincere words and seeing that beautiful sparkling ring, it erased any of my disappointment.

About a week later, Mason and I were at his house discussing what wedding details were left to plan. He began telling me about a conversation he'd had with one of his friends. He said his friend was happy that Mason was getting remarried after losing his former spouse. Then he shared how his friend thought he was moving too fast and wondered if he had taken the appropriate amount of time to heal and to date. I felt that icy chill start to creep down my spine, but I just listened before acting on my emotions.

"Lomasi, I told him I love you and I believe you are my soul mate," Mason explained. "I told him our connection is like no other. If someone hasn't experienced this type of connection, they would never understand."

He said he told his friend how the children loved me, and how I had their best interest at heart. I felt so

Unqualified: The Ineligible Bachelor

relieved! *Whew!* I sure thought he was going to have a flip-flop moment. I suddenly felt warm and fuzzy and the icy chill melted away. I was so proud we were going forward with the marriage. I felt confident that Mason had my back.

"Lomasi, do you think we are moving too fast? Do you want to wait some more time? I mean, what's the rush?"

And just like that, the icy chill was back. In a matter of three minutes, every bit of peace and relief I had was snatched from my soul. I immediately interrupted him and told him no, we were moving forward as planned. I saw how easily he was influenced by other's opinions; he didn't seem to have much backbone. I was now worried that my dream from the year prior was going to really happen. That on our wedding day, Mason would say he wasn't ready. *Father, take the wheel.*

The week of the wedding, I was busy with last-minute details. One of the things I wanted to do was dance for Mason at the reception, so I needed to work on choreography to a gospel song. I had been involved in dance ministry since my twenties. It was really strong in my spirit to do that for my husband-to-be. He had never seen me dance for the Lord, and I was happy to bless him with something so sacred.

Mr. Dawaitis Over

I was faced with a truly unsettling moment that week. We were out with the kids, and I had to stop at a craft store to pick up some materials for the wedding. Mason and I were excitedly talking about the villa that came with our wedding package, and Tammy and Tre jumped into our conversation.

They were excited too and began using terms like "our hotel room." *Nope, it is not your room, young ones. You will be staying with your aunt,* I said in my head and then out loud since Mason didn't clarify it for them. I was left to explain that all of us wouldn't be sleeping together the night of the wedding. They got so upset. Tammy, who was fourteen at the time, started to cry. (That was a manipulation tool she used with her daddy.) Mason just left me out there to sink!

"Can't they stay the night with us?" he asked me in front of the children.

I later discovered that was his manipulation tool he used with me when he was angry, tried to avoid conflict, or wanted to stay in the kids' good graces by pleasing them.

Is he kidding me right now? I thought. We were abstaining from sex until marriage so why on God's green earth would he want the children to sleep in the room with us on our wedding night?! Mason had a problem telling his children no, so I gave him the "look."

"Sorry guys. You won't be staying in the room with us on the night of the wedding," he finally answered. "I don't know what the big deal is!" he mumbled under his breath, but loud enough for Tammy and Tre to hear. Then he walked off with the kids.

Unqualified: The Ineligible Bachelor

That was such an uncomfortable conversation; he left me hanging there because he didn't have the guts to say no to his kids. Of course, it made me look mean and uncaring (a feeling that would soon become my new normal).

I had a private conversation with his auntie a few days before the wedding. I told her I didn't think Mason had completely cleared out his deceased wife's things from the master bedroom. There were also a lot of her items in the spare bedroom and in the garage. Since Mason had only five years left to pay off his home, I had agreed to move into his house with the promise we would remodel to make it my own.

I asked his aunt if she would remove his deceased wife's belongings from the home. She was concerned that Mason hadn't taken the time to do it but understood it needed to be done. She said she was going to have a talk with him and agreed to clear out the items while we were on our honeymoon.

Mr. Dawaitis Over

Two days before the wedding, my matron of honor hosted a bridal shower for me. Many of my wedding guests and soon-to-be family members, church family, and friends showed up. It was such a beautiful occasion, and I felt so special and loved. At the end, all the women laid hands on me and prayed over me. I felt God's peace and strength as the weekend drew closer.

After rehearsal on Saturday, my matron of honor and I walked the grounds, and I reflected on the "two becoming one," just like God's word said. The next day, I'd be married to my 'Adam.' Honestly, that's how I saw Mason because when I prayed in the beginning of our relationship, God led me to the Adam and Eve verses. I truly felt I was taken from Mason's rib and formed just for him. It was just a feeling I couldn't explain to anyone; either you had experienced it or you hadn't.

I woke up panicking on our wedding day, but it wasn't wedding jitters. I was anxious because I couldn't find a letter I had written Mason ten months prior as an act of faith. The letter expressed my love for him and my purpose in his life that God revealed to me. Also, I expressed that my love for God was greater, and I was taking a vow of obedience; if he was receiving the letter, it was only because of God's will on our wedding day. But now I couldn't find that letter anywhere!

My stomach was in knots, but I had to start getting ready. My hairstylist was coming any minute to do my hair. The stylist and makeup artist made me feel like a princess; everything was perfect—except Tammy hadn't shown up on time. She didn't arrive until thirty minutes before the wedding started and looked a mess.

I was so angry with her for not coming early as we had planned. I ended up scolding her and asked the stylist to do her hair after she put on her dress. Tammy got mad for two reasons: for being scolded and for having her hair put up in a style she didn't like. I noticed Mason's auntie was quiet and salty as well. I thought it was because of Tammy's shenanigans, but I later found out it was because I scolded Tammy.

The wedding was beautiful and all that I dreamed it would be. Mason and I were finally married! I was so happy that I got to enjoy this day. The dance I performed for Mason was beautiful, and there wasn't a dry eye at the reception. It was truly the best day ever.

After our wedding night, we grabbed breakfast and headed back home. I had to start packing up my apartment so I could move into Mason's house in a couple of weeks. In looking back, I realize that I packed and moved a lot of my things by myself. A moving company transported my large belongings, but Mason offered little help during the move. One day while I was packing, Mason called.

"Hey, Lomasi. What's going on?"

"Ah, packing up my apartment," I said looking at my phone with my "really?" face.

"Oh, okay. Well, pack a few things for Puerto Rico. We leave tomorrow night."

"Oh, my gosh!" I shouted excitedly. "Wait, I thought you said we were staying local and going to Carlsbad this weekend. Mason, don't play with me."

"Surprise!"

I was so excited and switched from packing up my house to packing for our trip!

Mr. Dawaitis Over

While at the airport waiting for our flight to board, Mason's auntie called him. I could tell from his reactions it wasn't good.

"It must not be meant for us to go on this trip!" he blurted out.

I couldn't understand why she would be calling that time of night, but she was watching the children while we went on our honeymoon. I figured it had something to do with them. I could see Mason was really upset by what she had shared on the phone.

"What? Why? What's going on?" I probed while my heart sank. That all too familiar icy chill was creeping back.

"That was Auntie and she said Tre was acting up really bad. He was bothering his sister and being disrespectful to my aunt. She doesn't know how to deal with him. She was scared, Lomasi." He paused. "I really need to get him some help."

Tre's behavior wasn't unusual to us, but it was new to his aunt. Mason tried to keep Tre's problems a secret, but he couldn't hide this. Tre was suffering from a mood disorder and ADHD. It would have never gotten diagnosed if I hadn't brought it up to Mason while we were dating.

Although Tre was prescribed medicine for both, Mason was in denial and really wanted his son to be on ADHD medicine only for school. Tammy and I tried to tell him Tre's behavior was night and day without it. He was very aggressive and many times violent without it. We had to hide all knives and sharp tools from him because of a really bad episode a year prior.

Interestingly enough, the violent episodes mostly occurred with his dad and toward anything his dad possessed. It was hardly ever toward his sister or any other family members. He had never displayed those behaviors toward me either.

"He tried to set his sister on fire," Mason whispered in disbelief.

"What!?"

"And, when my aunt went into his room and told him she was going to call me, he pulled out a hammer he had hidden in his room and tried to hit her with it. He tried to hit Auntie!" Mason said, two blinks from crying. "Lomasi, you know she didn't do anything to him to warrant that."

I was in complete shock; not because of Tre's behavior, but because of the aggression toward his sister and aunt—the two people to whom he was closest. Even though I was disappointed our trip might be called off, I understood how Mason felt. It sucked because he'd been in such denial about Tre, and now it was spilling over into other areas of his life and with other people. I later learned Mason told Tre he didn't have to take his medicine during the summer. That explained some of the violent episodes that occurred that summer in addition to this one.

"Well, how is he doing now?" I asked.

"She said he is calm now."

"So, what do you want to do? Do you want to cancel the honeymoon?" I asked.

"You know what—no. Let's go enjoy our honeymoon. We just got married a few days ago. Tre's calm now."

"Are you sure, Mason?"

"Yes, let's go to Puerto Rico!"

Thirty minutes later, we boarded our flight and were off to Puerto Rico. We arrived the next afternoon and

Mr. Dawaitis Over

got checked into our hotel. We grabbed some dinner and hung out at a local bar. In what should've been a night of intimate bliss between a husband and wife, I was weirdly met with rejection. I knew once we said our vows, I'd be able, willing, and ready—and I was.

This is what God intended it for and I wanted to enjoy it with my husband. So, I was initiating lovemaking, but he was being distant. He even yelled at me and told me to relax. I don't know too many men who turn down sex, but this was my husband! (Unfortunately, this was an issue for several months post wedding.)

For me, that rejection was hard and confusing. As I came to learn, emotionally Mason had a hard time accepting that it was okay to have sex now after hearing "no, we can't" so many times while we dated. Honestly, I felt it was a form of "payback" for all the months we practiced celibacy. Mason often felt rejected during those times.

There were some beautiful moments during our honeymoon as well as some painful disappointments. On our final day, Mason was quiet and very short with me. He was moody because he missed the children. I knew how it would play out. He would have a nasty attitude, which would result in an argument due to his own guilt—but he would project all his ill temper onto me.

Unqualified: The Ineligible Bachelor

Over the next few months, I had a hard time finding my place in Mason's family. I drove over an hour to work each morning and ninety minutes coming home. Most days I would get home to find Mason in front of the television asleep. Some days I would come in exhausted and start cooking, only to find Mason and the children eating fast food in the family room. They would eat right in front of me and act like I wasn't in the kitchen preparing dinner. That hurt so much, especially after driving in traffic and barely being able to keep my eyes open.

Intimacy was still inconsistent. I started noticing Mason would try to fall asleep before I did; he also wasn't showering regularly. Later, he told me it was so he "could get out of having sex with me." He dodged conversations about opening a bank account together and adding me on utility accounts. He said he didn't need my help and for me to just take care of my own bills.

The more I pressed the desire of being joined as one, the more he avoided it. I talked to God often and reminded him that he said I was to be his help meet, but Mason was rejecting me as his wife. A friend suggested I talk to other married women who had experienced similar problems. There was a distinct line drawn in our family: Mason, Tammy, and Tre on one side and me

Mr. Dawaitis Over

on the other. It became my new normal, and I didn't understand why.

I began comparing myself to his deceased wife since she was thrown in my face during adversity. I started to work harder to outdo whatever she did—whatever that was. Emotionally, I was breaking down. I even went to a therapist so I could make sense of everything, but nothing brought resolution or peace.

Sad, confused, and frustrated, I finally shared my feelings with Mason. I spoke about our sex life: me always initiating it and him rejecting me, blaming it on the psychological effects he claimed to suffer from being celibate during our courtship. I explained how I felt disconnected from him, Tammy, and Tre, especially when he would buy meals for the three of them when he knew I would be coming home to cook dinner. Then they would sit and eat in front of me without offering me any food.

I also mentioned how I was shamed when I bought household items, such as a toaster, new curtains, or even got the carpets shampooed. Mason would say I thought I was better than what they already had in the home or that things weren't good enough for me—in front of Tammy and Tre. Sometimes the children even questioned me. I was always defending myself.

After church one Sunday, we all went to breakfast and Mason brought up some of what I had shared with him. We hadn't discussed sharing it with the children or whether I would feel comfortable for him to address it in front of me.

"Hey guys, we are going to have a family meeting," he started. "Lomasi is feeling disconnected from the family.

Unqualified: The Ineligible Bachelor

What are some things you can think of for her to do to feel a part of the family?" he asked the kids.

I was burning up. *He just asked these kids what I can do to feel like part of the family!* I felt so humiliated.

"Well, she could do more chores," Tre offered.

"Not talk on the phone," Tammy added.

Mason said absolutely nothing and left me to fend for myself. I don't know why I felt the need to defend myself to a twelve year old and a fourteen year old, but I suppose it was because my husband didn't have my back. Unfortunately, that was something else I would experience frequently.

After four months of marriage, I brought up "being one" again and how important it was to me. Mason knew this because we attended a premarital course together three weeks before we got married. He looked at me and that icy chill began to creep down my spine.

"Lomasi, I've had a change of heart. I made a mistake in marrying you. I think we should get a divorce."

"The devil is a liar!" I yelled. "He will not destroy what God brought together!"

From that moment on, it was solidified. I was alone and married. I lived in a home where I was treated like an unwanted guest and a nanny to the children. Except for an emerging sex life and some small talk, I cooked, cleaned, and helped the children with homework.

We spent our first-year anniversary in a couple's counseling session. Things started to improve in many ways but not in others. We attended marriage workshops and a couple's life group (similar to a group Bible study). We attended a financial class together that I thought was to help us come together financially, but that wasn't Mason's intention.

During a doctor's visit, I found out I needed surgery on my leg. Mason took me to the hospital and stayed until I was in recovery. The doctor explained I would need to be out of work for about a week and prohibited me from unnecessary walking and climbing stairs. That meant I would need a lot of assistance because the bedrooms were on the second floor and the kitchen was on the first.

Mason didn't want to take time off work, so he called a neighbor to see if his wife, Rosie—whom I had never met—could come help me. I felt so abandoned once again! I needed help walking to the bathroom, sitting on the toilet, getting into the bath, and getting in and out of the bed.

Rosie ended up being a godsend. She blessed me in so many ways, nursing me back to health, physically and emotionally. She offered a listening ear and shared conversations about God and his word. As Mason's neighbor, Rosie even gave me some insight into Mason, his personality, his presence in his first marriage, and family or lack thereof. She also told me a little about Tammy and Tre because her daughter had babysat them.

God is so intentional. He knew I needed this woman in my life at that time because Mason was not qualified

Unqualified: The Ineligible Bachelor

to be the husband God had called him to be. Rosie and I became good friends, and she was an influential person in my life for several years.

"I don't know if I am in love with her. I don't know if I ever was," Mason admitted to the therapist. "Maybe I was just trying to replace what I lost."

That icy chill went through my body for the umpteenth time. Mason's words struck me in the heart again. I don't know how many times he had used the divorce word to try to manipulate me since we had been married four months ago.

"Oh, really? So, you used me?" I fired back.

"I do love you, but I am not sure I'm in love with you," he explained. "I had no business getting married. I just didn't want to lose you. But the truth is, I'm still grieving and in a lot of pain. My kids are still grieving and having a tough time, too," Mason explained. "I wasn't in the right state of mind."

"Mason, before I said yes to marrying you, I asked you if you had dealt with your grief and were ready. You were so confident that you were. As a matter of fact, you assured me you'd had a lot of time to think, reflect, and release. And that you had spent some time talking to "her" and closing that book. You said you were ready!" I yelled. I was so irritated.

"Despite how it affects us, Lomasi, this is Mason's truth. He and I can work this out some more in one-on-one sessions," the therapist chimed in during an uncomfortable silence.

"Well, what am I supposed to do with my feelings in the meantime, huh?" I asked angrily.

"Well … I don't know," the therapist responded.

You don't know? So, the couple's therapist cannot provide counsel right now. Good to know, I thought.

"Okay," I replied numbly. I obviously needed to find my own therapist to help me deal with this new bomb Mason just dropped on me. Mason continued to see this therapist, and I found a new one that Rosie recommended.

With my new counselor, Brittany, I learned a lot about me and my marriage. I really enjoyed talking to her. She helped me put a lot of things into perspective. One of my struggles was being married to a man who said he wasn't in love with me, but remaining physically intimate despite feeling rejected and manipulated.

Brittany helped me see I was in an emotionally abusive marriage. Mason manipulated me by threatening divorce, not wanting to come together financially, or using the children. The emotional abuse was one of my therapist's main concerns. She offered me healing, personal growth, and communication activities—but she never suggested divorce.

My fortieth birthday was a few months away, and I wanted to have a milestone birthday party. I decided on a masquerade theme. Mason wasn't happy about it at all.

Unqualified: The Ineligible Bachelor

However, he had gone all out for Tammy's sweet sixteen birthday party earlier in the year. He told me she should get whatever she wanted when I reminded him of the budget.

Mason told me he wasn't on board with having a party for me and didn't understand why we just couldn't go to dinner instead. So, I decided to throw a party for myself. I designed my invitations and reserved the venue. One of the children's cousins helped me plan it.

I asked Mason if my mom, sister, and two of my best friends from Boston coming in for the party could stay with us. He said he was cool with it, but the bathroom wasn't up to par for guests. He said it needed to be remodeled so the next week he brought in a contractor who said the remodel would be done before my party.

Four days before my party and my family and friends would be flying into town. I was out shopping for additional bath towels and washcloths, bathroom mirrors that needed to be installed the next day and a couple of accessories for the bathrooms. I called Mason from *Home Goods* and he was acting very nasty towards me and was rushing me off the phone because he was talking to his aunt. Obviously he was in a mood.

Chris, who was visiting us the weekend before my party, called me as I was coming home from shopping to tell me about Mason's mood. He said Mason had a problem with him lying across the bed while he was watching football in our bedroom. Chris said Mason told him to sit on the floor because the bed is "where it goes down" and "it isn't a good look for a man to be lying on another man's bed." *Why would he even have that type of conversation with my son? That was so inappropriate and disrespectful.*

Mr. Dawaitis Over

That evening, Mason and I came home from a church event, and he was still in a weird mood. He acted like he wanted to get something off his chest. That's when he decided to call a family meeting. The last time, I was blindly brought into a conversation that didn't go well; I was nervous this was going to be the same.

He called everyone to the table and began addressing his disappointment with each child. The list ranged from Tammy's bad attitude, Tre's disrespect, and the issue involving my son lying across the bed. He then turned to me.

"And you!" he yelled.

I cut him off. "Mason if there's anything you want to discuss with me, let's talk outside. I'm not one of the children."

"I don't want to go outside! That's what I mean. Nobody respects me in this house. I am tired of it! All I want is some respect. I am the king of this house. I am the only one paying the motherf*****g bills. So, if anyone has a problem with what I said, they can get the f*ck out!" he blared.

My blood began boiling and I lost it. "You pay the bills because you want to pay them. I can pay the bills, but you won't let me. You don't want to be one with me!" I yelled. "Where are they? Put me on the account. I have been waiting to pay!"

"Oh yeah! I know you want to take control!" he shouted.

I stood up. "I'm not going to sit here and let you disrespect me by talking to me like I'm one of these kids," I said, while walking to the kitchen.

Unqualified: The Ineligible Bachelor

He followed behind me still hollering. Next thing I know, I picked up the skillet containing our dinner and threw it. Ground beef went everywhere. As Mason turned around, the pan grazed his elbow and left a nick the size of a paper cut.

"Call the police!" he yelled. "She hit me with the pan. I am bleeding!"

Chris stepped in and tried to get the two adults to calm down. He really did his best, but the both of us were past that point now.

"No Chris, your mom walks around here like she's a queen b**ch grabbing her balls!" Mason shouted.

Before I could say anything else, my son beat me to it.

"I was trying to help calm you two down, because obviously emotions are running high," he said. "You called my mama a b**ch? You ain't going to disrespect my mom like that in front of me! Now this is where I draw the line. Let's go outside, homie!"

"Chris, I didn't call her a b**ch! I said she walks around like one," Mason answered.

"Outside homie!" Chris opened the door, walked outside, and stood in the street.

"You threw a pan at me, and now your son wants to fight me!" Mason blurted out.

I went upstairs to the bedroom to separate myself from the situation. I called Rosie to see if she and her husband could come over and help diffuse this madness.

While I was upstairs, I heard unfamiliar voices downstairs. I looked out the window and saw Chris sitting on his car still waiting for Mason to come outside. There was also a police car out front. Great! Someone had called

Mr. Dawaitis Over

the police! Minutes later, one of the officers came upstairs to talk to me.

He told me that because Mason had a nick on his arm, he would have to arrest me if Mason decided to press charges. He also explained that since I was a schoolteacher, it would jeopardize my teaching license. The officer said he would talk to Mason again.

Mason didn't press charges, but the officer asked if Chris and I could leave the house for the night to let cooler heads prevail. Rosie and her husband offered for us to stay with them. My son and I grabbed our belongings and walked toward the door.

"I didn't press charges. I saved you!" Mason screeched. "And get my key from your son. He isn't welcome here!"

That was the beginning of one of the darkest periods of my life. Rosie confided in me that Mason told the cops he was planning to file for divorce on September 25, two days after my 40th birthday. Rosie said the police officer asked Mason if he had planned this ordeal. He had answered no, but Rosie and I both felt it was possible since he was a master manipulator.

When I returned to the house the next day, I moved into the guest bedroom. I didn't speak to Mason or the children. I was numb; I felt dead inside. I didn't know how

I was going to hide this from my mom and sister when they arrived for my party in a couple of days.

My mom, sister and best friends were planning to arrive late the next evening. I was so excited. While at work I texted Mason to see if I could use his SUV to pick them up. He told me no. I had to leave work early to rent an SUV for the day so all their luggage would fit.

The night I picked up my family and friends at the airport, boy, did I wear the mask well! No one sensed anything was wrong until the next day. My mom noticed Mason and the "atmosphere" at home felt cold. The children weren't very sociable either. I tried to play it off. We still had to finish some last-minute details for the birthday party, so I got the ladies busy with those.

I went upstairs and asked Mason if he was attending the party. He said no, he didn't want my son and any goons to threaten him if he came. Another dagger to my wounded heart. I thought Mason would go to save face in front of my family and friends. I was devastated.

The morning of the party, Mom and I went downtown to the Flower District to pick up mini white roses for my centerpieces. I don't think we were five minutes into the drive when she looked over at me and asked:

"Okay, what's going on? I know something is up."

"Oh, I'm just in my thoughts about getting older," I told her. I didn't want to tell her the truth because she wouldn't be able to handle it.

"Oh, okay. Are you sure?"

"Yes," I tried to reassure her.

As we headed back home, I started feeling lightheaded and seeing black spots and they were increasing. I truly

Mr. Dawaitis Over

felt like I was getting ready to black out any moment! I asked my mom to drive the rest of the way because I wasn't feeling well. When we got home, I went to the bedroom to lie down. As soon as I reached the bathroom, I had a breakdown and couldn't stop crying. I crawled from the bathroom to the bed and continued to cry uncontrollably.

Everything I'd been holding in over the past week—months really—came to the surface and I just crashed. One of my friends heard me crying and came to check on me. I told her briefly what happened the night I almost got arrested and how Chris was banned from the house for the drama Mason had created. She was livid. Soon, another friend came in and told me she was getting a hotel for all of us so we could be comfortable and enjoy our last night together without any drama. My sister came in last. I showed her the police report from that night and told her what happened. She was also furious.

I managed to pull myself together and we packed up the car with the many containers of decorations and luggage in time for my party. It was everything I had imagined. A coworker provided live music at the very last second as a favor to me. They were beyond amazing. Everyone had a great time and I was even able to enjoy it.

At some point, Mason showed up like he was a knight in shining armor. It was hard for me to be fake after everything I had experienced with him over the past week. He left after thirty minutes, probably because I didn't pay any attention to him.

I headed home the next morning after staying at the hotel with my family and friends. I went upstairs to the guest room and crawled into bed—my safe haven during the next several months. My world got darker and darker by the day. No more masks, literally and figuratively, and no more pretending. Just plain numbness.

My depression worsened the longer I stayed in that house. The best way I can explain it is I was a zombie ... just walking dead. Mason would sometimes come into the room while I was sleeping, and his presence would terrify me. If he tried to approach me, I would have an anxiety attack. I took medicine to help me sleep. I started getting sick and my blood levels dropped; I was weak and fatigued. My nerves were so on edge I started locking the bedroom door so I wouldn't wake up startled with Mason hovering over me.

One day, Mason asked me how long I was going to keep this act up. I explained that it wasn't an act, and that my therapist said I was suffering from post-traumatic stress disorder and depression. What made it even harder was my son's apartment lease was coming to an end, and he had nowhere to go.

Mason kept harassing me and causing more anxiety attacks. I finally asked if he wanted to sit in on one of my therapy sessions to learn about what I was going through. I was hoping then he would leave me alone and stop trying to make small talk with me.

Brittany explained to Mason what was going on with me and the causes and effects. He told her he didn't believe it and that I was a good actress. He asked how long it would take for me to get over it. She told him she could not answer that. Mason boasted about his first marriage, how successful it was, and how he took his vow "in sickness and in health 'til death do us part" serious. He had stayed faithful and supportive until his first wife died.

"Your current wife is sick!" Brittany asserted. "Just because she doesn't have a physical illness doesn't mean she's not sick. She's emotionally and mentally sick. You need to give her time and support her through what she is going through—if, in fact, you are taking your vow seriously."

"I can't bear to look at her walk around blank," Mason confessed. "She gets anxious just from my presence! She comes into the house and doesn't speak to anyone and goes to 'her room.' She sleeps in the guest bedroom! I don't want to hurt her any more than what I have. If she doesn't snap out of it, then I don't want to be in a marriage like this," he threatened.

"Mason, she has created a safe place for herself away from the ones who have caused her trauma and pain. It is going to take some time. Give her the space she needs and respect her boundaries," Brittany suggested.

As time went on, I grew worse on the outside but was content in my bubble. I was spiritually dead and stopped reading the Bible. I couldn't pray or utter God's name. One day, Mason told me he filed divorce papers because he didn't want to cause me any more pain. He asked if I wanted to sign them. I told Mason I would sign them, but I needed counsel to look them over because I was not familiar with legal jargon. He said he was just joking and wanted to see what I would say. I remained numb and blank.

Brittany was still concerned about my overall health and suggested I go away for a day or two to do some self-reflecting and feeling activities. She also thought it would be good for me to remove myself from the house for a few days.

I found a cute casita in Las Vegas and booked it for a weekend. I completed the assigned activities from Brittany; it was emotionally tough, but it was liberating. I departed for Los Angeles with two things: a sense of peace and the possibility of being able to have small talk with Mason. But when I got back "home," it hit me all over again. I was back to feeling numb and dead inside; into my tomb I went.

A couple of weeks later, Brittany gave me new assignments, and I went away again. Mason wasn't happy about it, but that didn't stop me. I was on the search to find peace again. By now, I had totally disengaged from the family, and the casita was the one place where I knew I could find peace.

Over the course of the next month, I continued having frequent anxiety attacks. I thought they were from being in the house, but I also had them when Chris and I went to Boston to celebrate his birthday and be with our family for Christmas.

At that point, my mother sat me down and I had to come clean about everything. Thinking back, that must have been so hard watching your child crumble emotionally before your eyes. On the advice of my mom and Rosie, I agreed it would be best for me to move out of the house. I also invited Chris to move in with me since his lease was expiring soon.

When I got back to Los Angeles, I signed a lease for a new apartment, received the keys, and headed to the house

Mr. Dawaitis Over

to tell Mason and the children. With the help of Rosie and her husband, I moved out of the house two days later. Mason actually offered to help, which I didn't expect; I figured it was because his friend, Rosie's husband, was helping and Mason didn't want to look bad. Whatever the motive, I was grateful.

I was excited about this new change in my life. I was officially separated from Mason, Tammy, and Tre. Immediately, I felt at peace in this new space. I started attending church with Rosie and her husband. I think I cried at each service. God wasn't through with me after all.

As I was getting settled in my apartment, I had the biggest yearning to talk to God. It had been four long months. The more I spent time with him and prayed, the more pain and chains were released from me. He delivered me from every bitter, angry, sad, depressed, rejected, and unworthy feeling I had suffered since that traumatizing event the week before my birthday. Truthfully, I'd say even way before then.

I forgave Mason for his transgressions against me. I asked God to forgive me for holding on to those feelings and making a home for them for so long. I apologized for my behavior toward Mason and the children. I literally felt a weight lifted. It was one of the most liberating God moments I ever experienced.

One day I saw an announcement at church for Beth Moore's *Breaking Free* Bible study. I called Rosie and asked her opinion about whether I should take the class. She encouraged me to go, saying it could help me stay in a place of freedom and get more of what God had in store for me.

Unqualified: The Ineligible Bachelor

I began attending the class every Saturday morning. It was amazing! God was just downloading into me. I also met new friends who attended the church. I was even able to start having cordial conversations with Mason, and I began sharing my progress with him.

About a month later, I was diagnosed with pneumonia. I was running a fever and was extremely sick. I went to a doctor's appointment for the symptoms. I don't know how I made it there, but it was definitely by God's grace. By the time I got into the office, I was burning up with 104-degree fever and couldn't walk. I was out of it. I was called into a room pretty quickly and once I sat on the table my eyes immediately closed.

A nurse came in to tell me that she called Mason two hours ago to inform him on what was going on and asked him if he was able to come and bring me to the hospital. Mason arrived about six hours passed the time I arrived and the office was closed. All the staff had left and the after-hours doctor was in.

Mason drove me to Cedar Sinai Hospital. He stayed with me throughout the wee hours in the morning despite his feelings toward me. Later that morning, I called Chris to tell him what was going on. He came to the hospital too, and he and Mason were cordial to one another.

Mason showed up again the day I was discharged, five days later, and stayed about thirty minutes. I didn't hear from him after that until two weeks later. He said he hadn't been by to check on me because "he had other priorities to take care of." Obviously, caring for his sick wife wasn't a priority. So much for "taking his wedding vows seriously."

Mr. Dawaitis Over

I continued to pray for Mason during my recovery, but I had to learn how to take care of myself. I was still on strong medications and doing breathing treatments around the clock. The one thing that remained consistent in my life was God. I spent hours with him and continued the *Breaking Free* Bible study on my own at home.

God was speaking loud and clear about me, Mason, and our marriage. He also used some amazing people, even angels, to love on me and care for me when my husband wouldn't. After a while, Mason stopped by occasionally claiming he missed me and wanted to spend time with me. It appeared the real motive was sex, regardless of the fact I was still trying to recover from pneumonia.

After a lengthy recovery and I was back at work, Mason told me he had filed divorce papers. He informed me a server had come to my apartment repeatedly. Mason thought I was trying to dodge him, which was ridiculous since I didn't even know he had filed in the first place.

I decided to opt out of my apartment lease early when I found out a toxic fume that had come into my unit a few months earlier could have caused my pneumonia. I began my search for a new apartment, but I was having a hard time trying to find one. Supposedly, Mason's server had stopped trying to issue me the divorce papers; Mason believed it was a sign for me to move back in with him.

I told him Chris would have to come with me since he didn't have a place to stay now. I thought Mason had moved past that horrible night since he was "forced" to speak to Chris at the hospital, but he hadn't. That was the newest hurdle I had to climb.

Ironically, I got approved for an apartment I liked. The day I was notified and supposed to sign the lease, Mason told me he wanted me to move back in again and asked me not to sign. He wanted to have a family meeting about what life would be like if Chris and I moved back.

I didn't sign the lease as an act of faith in God. I believed he was getting ready to restore my marriage. We decided to have the family meeting with all the children present. When Chris and I arrived, Mason chickened out and we all sat there for two hours waiting for him to start the conversation. He and I finally went upstairs to talk privately.

"Mason, what's the deal?" I started. "We've all been sitting for two hours watching you watch television. The kids are tired."

"I'm sorry, Lomasi. Seeing you here with Chris brought up some deep emotions," he confessed. "I'm still hurt by Chris's actions toward me from that night. I'm not able to forgive him. And I'm hurt by your moving out," he said tearing up. "I've changed my mind about your moving back here." And with that he handed me his wedding band.

Mr. Dawaitis Over

He made me lose out on an apartment so now it was back to the drawing board. By this time, I was in heavy conversation with God, because I couldn't understand what was going on. I wasn't sure if I could ever trust Mason's word again. This was such an emotional setback.

I extended my lease an additional thirty days, but I still wasn't able to find another apartment. A week later, Mason called to ask how the search was going. *I wouldn't even be in this boat if I didn't fall for your wishy-washy ways,* I thought.

"It's going," I responded. "I still haven't found anything."

"Lomasi, just move back. I am sorry that I changed my mind last week. I feel bad that I caused you to lose that apartment," he said apologetically. "You know I love you and would be miserable without you," he admitted. "I have to work on my emotions. I have to confess, I'm still hurt that you left the first time and walked away from the marriage."

I really didn't believe him and didn't know if I could trust him anymore. I told him yes, but I kept searching anyway. I wasn't going to have a repeat of what had just happened. My apartment management company already stated they wouldn't approve another lease extension.

Unqualified: The Ineligible Bachelor

I eventually did see an apartment I liked and decided to apply. Everything went well, but they miscommunicated the security deposit information. It was double the rent. I knew I didn't have that, so I checked back in with Mason. He still seemed to be in a good headspace. I declined the apartment and called a moving company to move my belongings back to Mason's. The day before the move Mason called to check in.

"Hey, how's it going?" he asked.

"It's going well. I'm all packed."

"Oh, wow …" he paused. "Lomasi, I'm not ready. I changed my mind."

"I'm not doing this with you!" I cut him off. "I have a truck scheduled to be here in the morning. They'll be moving my belongings. The management company isn't giving me any more extensions. This isn't a game. I'm going to be homeless, Mason!"

"Well, I don't feel comfortable with you coming."

"Well, I don't know what to tell you because I'm coming."

"I don't want you to come!" he demanded. "So, you're just going to disrespect my feelings?"

"At this point, Mason, it is what it is. I'm about to be homeless messing with you. And technically that's still my home too. We aren't divorced. See you tomorrow, Mason." I hung up the phone pissed yet feeling empowered.

The next day I arrived at the house, unlocked the door with my key, and walked in. I said hello to Mason, Tammy, and Tre, who were watching television in the family room. Mason looked like he had seen the "Ghost from Christmas Past" from *A Christmas Carol*. He got up and followed me to the door, only to see the moving truck parked outside and movers unloading my belongings.

"I can't believe you just showed up like this," he said.

"I can't believe you changed your mind in less than twenty-four hours before I was scheduled to move back here knowing I couldn't extend my lease," I fired back.

"I don't feel comfortable with this, and you're disrespecting me and my kids."

"I don't feel comfortable with the thought of you not caring that your wife would've been homeless," I said as I continued to direct the movers.

As the movers started to bring items into the house, Mason told them to put my furniture in the formal living room. He allowed them to take a large armoire upstairs and leave it in the hallway. Mason made it clear he didn't want me to get "comfortable" so I wouldn't stay long. He also declared my son couldn't move in until Chris apologized for his behavior on "that night" when Chris threatened to fight Mason for calling me a b**ch.

Unfortunately, I lived separately from Mason, Tammy, and Tre again. I tried to keep a gentle and kind spirit, but they didn't interact much with me. It was almost like Mason told them to stay away from me. I cooked for everyone, but they all turned down the food. I made a prayer area in the closet because I knew I was going to have to stay in constant prayer.

I was running up credit card bills paying for Chris to stay in a hotel. I told Mason he and Chris needed to have their talk soon, and he agreed to it. The conversation went well, and Chris was allowed to move in, but he had to sleep on the couch. The atmosphere was still awkward and uncomfortable.

Unqualified: The Ineligible Bachelor

A short time later, Chris found out he needed emergency surgery on his shoulder from an accident a few weeks earlier. The surgery was scheduled for the next week. I told Mason that Chris would need an actual bed to recover in, so I suggested we move him to the guest bedroom. The recovery time would be about three months.

Mason vetoed that request and said Chris would have to stay on the couch. *What kind of person would refuse his stepson a place to recover after having a major surgery?* I had to go into the prayer closet because of the evil and bitter spirit that persisted in Mason.

The day before the surgery, I decided to set up the bed. Mason was pissed when he saw it.

"You just continue to disrespect me," he huffed and walked off.

"Actually, I can't imagine someone having major shoulder surgery and having to recover on a couch. That's just so insensitive," I responded.

As Chris recovered over the next couple of months, I realized I couldn't trust Mason to help care for him. One day when I went to church, I asked Mason to help Chris with medication should he need it for pain; he said he would. When I got home, Chris said Mason hadn't come in one time to check on him, and when Chris asked Mason to help him with his pain medicine, he never did.

That broke my heart. But what did I expect? Mason couldn't even help me, his own wife, during my sickness. Even though Mason and I continued to have conversations, the environment was still unsettling. I wasn't treated as a wife or supported emotionally. I continued to pursue and press God for peace and change. *Your will be done, Lord.*

Mr. Dawaitis Over

In November, Mason went to Miami for his birthday weekend. When he came back, he was acting differently toward me. Maybe his getaway was what he needed. *Maybe God talked to him while he was there.* I rolled with the changes and began to see some light at the end of the tunnel. I cooked a Thanksgiving dinner and everyone enjoyed themselves. Things seemed to be getting back to normal. I felt like I could finally exhale.

Christmas was quickly approaching, and home life was still stable. I came home from work one afternoon and began preparing dinner. I was talking to Mason from the kitchen and he interrupted me.

"Lomasi? Did you hear someone at the door?"

"No," I answered over the sound of running water. "I didn't hear anything. I have the water on."

"I think someone is at the door," he continued from his favorite recliner.

"Okay. Well, I can't get it because I'm cleaning chicken. Can you go check?"

"Are you Lomasi Thompson?" an unfamiliar voice asked.

I slowly looked up at the stranger standing two feet away. Before I could focus on his face, he handed me a thick manila envelope.

"You've been served."

That icy chill was back. Every negative emotion God had delivered me from several months ago resurfaced. I rebuked those feelings and asked God to give me strength. Mason was nowhere to be seen. *Of course.* I finished cooking, ate my dinner, cleaned up, and went to bed searching for peace.

Unqualified: The Ineligible Bachelor

"Lomasi, say something," Mason appealed, from his side of the bed.

There was nothing at this point to talk about. I was betrayed—again.

For the next three months, our lawyers battled over requests and demands. "Evil Mason" was back and made life trying and stressful. At one point, he called me a "gold-digging b**ch." *Please! After all I had to deal with: you and your wishy-washiness, your narcissistic, manipulating ass, and your lack of emotional and physical support. I still had remained in prayer and committed to this marriage.* When we finally reached an agreement, I moved out and never looked back.

Mason was unqualified to be my husband. He was still grieving his deceased wife, he felt stuck in the middle between his children and me (he told me he'd always choose them over me), he wasn't able to forgive my son and me and move forward, he didn't trust me, he was manipulative and wishy-washy, he always wanted to play the victim in marital adversity, and he was emotionally and verbally abusive.

Sure, we had great chemistry and an unreal connection with one another. But Mason didn't know how to love unconditionally. I do believe our marriage was ordained. But what God brought together, man unfortunately put asunder. I believe Mason loved me the best way he knew how from an already broken heart.

God taught me many lessons during my marriage to Mason. I learned patience, endurance, and how to love someone who had unlovable ways and wasn't qualified to return it. He taught me about forgiveness and grace repeatedly. He also showed me how to bridle my tongue. As

Mr. Dawaitis Over

my relationship with God grew deeper and my faith became stronger, I learned how to fight my battles—on my knees.

God doesn't play with marriage. He won't stand for a wife to be mistreated by her husband. There are consequences. I don't know if Mason is dealing with those repercussions here on earth, but I know he'll have to answer for his actions one way or another.

To this day, Mason blames me for ending the marriage by signing the divorce papers—that he served me. It is so sad, but true. I have forgiven Mason and keep him lifted in prayer. His personal struggles, insecurities, and pride kept him unqualified to love and cherish me, God's beloved gift.

"In the same way, you husbands must give honor to your wives. Treat your wife with understanding as you live together. She may be weaker than you are, but she is your equal partner in God's gift of new life. Treat her as you should so your prayers will not be hindered." (1 Peter 3:7, NLT)

"First pride, then the crash—the bigger the ego, the harder the fall." (Proverbs 16:18, MSG)

"For you know when your faith is tested, your endurance has a chance to grow." (James 1:3, NLT)

Ineligible Bachelor #7:
Mr. Prince Charming

At one time or another, we all wish our Prince Charming would come in and sweep us off our feet, thereby rescuing the damsel in distress.

I met my Prince Charming right before an extremely dark season of my life that was filled with depression and egged on by betrayal. You read all about that time in my life in Chapter 6. Prince Charming came in on his white horse and saved me—so to speak.

I met Prince Charming (that is what I actually called him because of how he came into my life) a month before my fortieth birthday. He was an IT guy who came to work on our computers at school. He seemed to spend more time than normal working on the computers in my classroom, but I did not think much about it at the time.

Most of the time he sat quietly working on the computers, but eventually my classroom helper and I started incorporating him into our conversations. One day, we started talking about music and he mentioned that he played the keyboard, played for all different artists, and produced and recorded music.

A light bulb went off in my head. I asked if he had a studio he could recommend because I wanted to record a rap for my birthday party. I told him I wanted to challenge myself and do something different that I had never done. He told me he had a studio set up at his house.

I didn't think there was any harm because a woman who came to the school on occasion introduced herself to me as his wife. I figured she'd be present. After we discussed how much he would charge for the session, Prince and I arranged studio time.

The studio area was off of the living room and had all of this equipment that seemed a bit intimidating to me. I had given him the name of the song a few days before the session. As soon as I sat down, he started playing the music on his keyboard. It had a jazz-flare that I wasn't expecting, but I was impressed nonetheless.

Let me start by saying, recording is not as easy as it looks! I'd been dancing and acting since a young age, but suddenly I was nervous and shy.

"Okay, start flowing," he said, while playing the music. "Let me hear how you sound."

"What?! Wait, I'm not a rapper. I don't know how to just flow," I responded. "Remember, I said I was doing this to challenge myself for my fortieth."

I started by reading the lyrics to the rhythm of the song as he played. But when he asked me to step to the mic, I froze up again. We took a break so I could calm my nerves and drink a glass of wine. *I can see why many musicians drink and smoke weed in the studio or before a performance. Geesh!*

Mr. Prince Charming

During the break, I learned that the woman I met at my school wasn't his wife, but they were in a "complicated dating relationship." She had just moved out of state to give them both space to figure things out. He knew I was married because I wore my wedding ring at school.

After I finished the wine, I finally recorded a version we were both happy with and we wrapped up the session. I couldn't wait to hear the final copy when he was done editing.

He told me he wasn't going to charge me the session fee as a gift for my birthday. I think it was because he felt bad for me. I was a hot mess that day.

I continued to see Prince at work, and he would joke about my horrific studio session. One day when he stopped by my room, he noticed I was upset. He asked if everything was all right, and I told him about the big blow up between my husband, my son, and my bonus children. Prince got pissed at my husband for disrespecting me and validated my son's behavior saying that was what a son was supposed to do—protect his mother.

That conversation made me feel a little better about what happened. It got me through the remainder of my workday after having such a long night. Prince expressed his concern for me and my safety and asked if there was anything he could do. Although there really wasn't, out of genuine concern, he would email me a couple times a week to check on me.

When Prince came by my classroom a few days later, I was in a furious text argument with Mason. Mason wouldn't allow me to use his SUV to pick up my mom, sister, and friends from the airport when they flew in to celebrate my fortieth birthday. When I shared what was happening, Prince offered to pick up my family and friends from the airport, but he had a Prius and I knew the four ladies and their luggage would never fit.

He was so sincere about wanting to help, I asked if he would take my final payment to the venue so I could leave early to go rent an SUV. Without hesitation, he said yes, and a few hours later, Prince called me to say he had dropped off the check.

"Lomasi, if there's anything else I can help you with, please let me know. I will gladly do it," Prince Charming said on a phone call.

"No, this was such a huge blessing! Thank you so much for stepping in on short notice."

"Well, just know it is all set. I'm going to text you a picture of the receipt," he said.

When the picture of the receipt came in, I noticed the words "CASH." *I didn't pay with cash, I paid with check.* I called Prince back.

"Hey, I got the receipt. Thanks, again," I told him. "But, um …"

"Oh, if you're wondering why it says cash, it's because I paid the final balance as my birthday gift to you," Prince explained. "Happy Birthday, Lomasi. I hope you have the best birthday after what you've been through."

"What? Are you serious?" I asked, shocked. "What are you going to do with the check?"

"Nothing," he replied nonchalantly. "Rip it up. Enjoy your birthday."

I was speechless. Then I did something I shouldn't have done. I immediately compared him to my husband.

Mr. Prince Charming

Here was this stranger, with no emotional or physical ties to me, supporting me on one of the most important days of my life. Then there was my husband who was constantly trying to find ways to ruin it.

On the morning of my party, I told two of my friends about Prince and what he had done. I asked if they thought it would be too much if I asked him to play some jazz at the beginning of my party. They both told me to do whatever made me happy, so four hours before the party I called Prince to see if he was available. I asked him how much he would charge me for one hour of music during dinner.

"I got you," he said.

That evening, Prince showed up with two other men to accompany him. I actually had a band playing at my birthday. I was so surprised! My heart was so full that he came through for me again. He didn't even charge me for the band costs, and they played longer than an hour because the DJ was late. They were having such a good time they just wanted to stay and party with us. He literally was my "knight in shining armor." He would become the one light in my soon-to-be dark world.

Prince continued to go above and beyond for me and my family. The night of my party, he drove my sister and son to the hotel where we were staying since Chris had too much to drink. Prince even stayed with my son for a while to make sure he was okay. I didn't know it at the time, but Prince rented a room in the same hotel to make sure my family and I were safe and settled. The next morning, he drove Chris to get his car and then called to check on me.

The following week, on my actual birthday, Prince made a card for my students to sign and had them sing

Unqualified: The Ineligible Bachelor

Happy Birthday to me. It was such a kind gesture. When I got sick and found out my blood levels were low, he offered to take me to the doctor. When I returned to work, I was greeted with breakfast and orange juice on my desk every day for a week to help build my iron and potassium levels. I was in such a dark place that his acts of kindness helped me hold on.

Prince continued to check on me over the next several weeks as I slipped deeper into depression. I would wake up in the wee hours of the morning and drive to Prince's apartment to just be still or rest. He never rejected me and always made me breakfast and sometimes lunch. He'd often play music on his keyboard that would soothe my soul.

Although I was walking in darkness, and had stopped pursuing God, this one saying would often come to mind: "I have come to set the captives free." I felt like a captive. *Hmm ... Did God send him to set me free? Free from heartbreak and darkness? Was he my guardian angel?* I would ask myself. Through a hardened heart and feeling numb, I eventually started to enjoy Prince's attention and care.

We started to develop feelings for each other. I was going through so much emotionally with my marital problems. A relationship with Prince was not an option—and deep down he knew it. He apologized for his feelings and said he "knew better." But the pain in his eyes was noticeable. He began to pull back some and allowed me time to go through the wreckage of my disintegrating marriage.

Mr. Prince Charming

Eventually I separated from Mason and started spending time with God. He opened my eyes to so many things I was blinded to during the darkness. I asked him for forgiveness for my behavior and the emotional ties I had created with Prince. I asked God to remove him from my life if he was not meant to be there.

Two weeks later, Prince told me his contract with my school was not renewed and he had to move back to his home out of state. As sad as I was, I knew this was from God. Prince Charming was unqualified (ineligible, in this case) because I was married. I was someone else's wife.

A couple of years after my divorce, Prince Charming moved back to Los Angeles. I was happy to see my friend! He had gone through a marriage and, unfortunately, a divorce as well. He was the same old guy, very attentive and caring.

He continued to be a friend I could count on, helping me out several times when I was sick. Both of us were now free to pursue a relationship, but I wasn't ready for one and honestly had no desire. The timing wasn't right yet again for Prince Charming. I really needed to heal.

Unqualified: The Ineligible Bachelor

As I took my time to heal, I saw things with a "new pair of eyes." I realized the need for healing wasn't the sole reason I didn't want a relationship with Prince. It was me. There were things about his personality I didn't find attractive; I also didn't feel the chemistry. I didn't want to waste his time.

With God showing me my worth during this time, I knew he wasn't the one. He was unqualified because I knew my worth. My worth was "far above rubies."

"The spirit of the sovereign LORD is on me, because the LORD has anointed me to proclaim good news to the poor. He has sent me to bind up the brokenhearted, to proclaim freedom for the captives and release from darkness for the prisoners." (Isaiah 61:1, NIV)

"Who can find a virtuous and capable wife? She is more precious than rubies." (Proverbs 31:10, NLT)

Ineligible Bachelor #8:
Mr. Recen Lee Divorced
Part I

Have you ever had a person you cared about from your past—we're talking twenty-plus years ago—boomerang back into your life when you least expected it?

I have. I met him almost twenty-five years ago in North Carolina while visiting my great-aunt for a couple of weeks. I had just come out of a short-lived but intense relationship. It ended abruptly, and it was taking a toll on me emotionally. So, Chris, who was about three years old, and I headed south for some rest and relaxation.

One of my dear friends, Malea, who lived in the same town as my aunt, invited me to a get-together her friends were having. She introduced me to Paul, Antoinette, and Lee. We all immediately hit it off. Laughter is truly medicine for the soul. I wanted to go to the store, and Lee volunteered to take me because he knew the neighborhood.

I was so comfortable with Lee that it felt like I had known him for years. He was funny and upbeat, plus he

Unqualified: The Ineligible Bachelor

had this larger-than-life personality. He was a breath of fresh air, and I was quickly drawn to him. We hit it off so well that we hung out the next evening; we had a strong connection. He was twenty-one and I was twenty. This became a bond that would never break.

When I returned home from my trip, Lee and I continued getting to know one another. He worked nights at a hotel, and I'd stay up until the wee hours almost every night to talk to him on the phone. He called me Lomasi B. The "B" stood for absolutely nothing other than it had a hip-hop flair. I remember talking about Atlanta, Georgia, so much that we decided we were going to move there and be roommates. *How naïve of me to think that the chemistry we had would've stopped at roommates.*

He planned to attend college, and I was going to teach school. I don't know how it would've worked when I had a child I was bringing into the home. Nonetheless, those were our plans. Lee moved to Atlanta in 2000 and I was supposed follow shortly thereafter.

One Sunday morning in early 2000, I woke up to a small voice saying *"California."* Honestly, I think that was one of the first times I heard the voice of God speak to me.

"God, are you telling me to go to California?" I asked aloud.

The premonition was strong, and I investigated it. I talked to a few people and prayed about it. Eventually, I attended a huge job fair that consisted of school districts from all over the United States. I met with administrators from Atlanta Public Schools who offered me employment on a contingency. I also had nine offers from schools in southern California.

Mr. Recen Lee Divorced Part I

You may remember reading about this in chapter one. Over time, the feelings became stronger and stronger, and I decided to follow the urges and move to Los Angeles. I broke the news to Lee who had already been in Atlanta for a few months. He was devastated, and he stopped talking to me.

For the first nine years in L.A., I intermittently thought about Lee. I often wondered how he was doing, what he was doing, what he looked like, and all the what ifs. I had married and divorced Earl during this time, but I still thought about Lee from time to time.

Then Facebook happened. When I finally joined, one of the first people I reconnected with was Malea. I asked her how Lee was doing. I told her I missed our friendship and thought about him through the years. I don't know if she was even aware of how close we had grown. She said he was doing great; he had gotten married and just had a baby. It felt like life left my body when I heard those words. "That's nice," I said, feeling stunned. "Wow, good for him!"

After I had collected myself, I said, "Malea, I'd really love to talk to Lee and catch up, but I respect marital boundaries."

"Lomasi, girl. Let me reach out to him. I'll tell him that we reconnected on social media and that you asked about him," she offered.

Days later, Lee sent me a message on Facebook. I freaked out and was so excited I responded as soon as I read it. I told him I missed our friendship. We reminisced and got caught up on each other's lives through Facebook and even spoke on the phone a few times. Just like that, those familiar feelings resurfaced; but I was single in L.A., and he was married in Atlanta. And marriage trumps everything.

Unqualified: The Ineligible Bachelor

About seven years later, Lee reached out on Facebook to send me a belated birthday greeting. We caught each other up on our lives; but once again, the timing was off. I was now remarried (to Mason), and Lee had a four-year-old daughter and his son was seven. He told me he wanted to come to L.A. one day and hang out. I doubted he would come because, in my experiences, more people travel east than west. And just like that, another three years passed by without talking.

A few years later, after my divorce from Mason, Lee and I connected again. I texted him to ask if he could advise Chris, who was relocating to Georgia for work and to assist my stepdad who just purchased a new home, on areas where to look for an apartment. (My mom was diagnosed with cancer a few years prior and traveled back and forth between Boston and Georgia as often as she could.) Lee was happy to help. Chris ended up getting cold feet with the idea of relocating and unfortunately didn't make it to Georgia. I didn't talk to Lee after that.

Chris finally decided to relocate and moved about five months after his first attempt. Unfortunately, the job Chris had lined up turned out to be a fluke. Lee offered to help Chris find another job. I was so appreciative because I didn't want my son to give up and head back to Los Angeles without giving it a fair chance. I had interceded in prayer for so long, and I wasn't going to let the devil have his way. *Get thee behind, Satan!*

"Masi B!" Lee shouted in capital letters in a text message. I could imagine just how he said it too. "When's the next time you'll be in Atlanta?"

Mr. Recen Lee Divorced Part I

"Actually, I'm planning to come for Thanksgiving to visit my son and stepdad." (At this point, my mom had been diagnosed with cancer and was being treated in Boston. She traveled back and forth between Boston and Georgia as often as she could.)

"Hey, don't be a stranger. Make sure you hit me up when you're here," Lee said. "And somebody has a birthday coming up!" He always loved to show me he knew my birthday, but he was always a day or two early.

I texted Lee when I got to Atlanta, and he responded immediately saying we needed to get together. A few days had passed and still hadn't heard from him. Thanksgiving night, my phone buzzed with a text message from Lee. He asked how long I was going to be in town; I told him I was leaving in the morning. He said he was going to swing by in the next hour.

I was excited about seeing my friend but a little anxious because I would be meeting his family as well. . Lee wasn't tall and skinny with a mouth full of gold teeth like when I last saw him in our twenty's, but a forty-four-year-old grown man who had filled out. He looked good, but his features were a bit different from what I remembered. His children were in the car with their cousins watching television. His wife wasn't there.

We sat outside talking and reminiscing for over an hour. It was getting colder by the minute, but this moment was too special to end the conversation. Then Lee asked me a game-changing question.

"Did I tell you that I was divorced?"

My heart skipped a beat. Then the "warm and fuzzies" overtook me. I hadn't experienced those feelings in a long time.

"Umm, nope, you didn't. Lee, no! I'm so sorry to hear that!" I said empathetically.

The next hour, we stood sharing "divorce horror stories." Lee confessed something he had never told me. He had turned down going to a college in Washington, D.C., to move to Atlanta because I had persuaded him to go. He had family there, so it made sense. He said he was crushed when I chose to go to L.A. instead of Atlanta. He also reminded me that we were supposed to be roommates.

I was speechless. I had no idea of the choice he made back then. I felt so sad that I had let him down—especially when he had other options and plans.

"I let you get away the first time; I'm not letting you get away this time," he declared. And immediately the "warm and fuzzies" resurfaced. *Was God giving us a second chance?* I wondered. I didn't know if God was in it, but it was exciting. I hadn't had the desire to date anyone for the last year and a half since my divorce from Mason. I was content being single.

Two and a half hours later neither one of us wanted the conversation to end, but I needed to pack and get ready to head back to L.A. Lee said he would fly out to see me, and I hoped he meant it because I didn't want to wait another twenty years to see him again. I walked into the house like a sixteen year old girl who was just captivated by the presence of her teenage boy crush.

The next few weeks rocked my world. I had reconnected to someone who had been dear to my heart since I was twenty years old and whom I never thought I'd see again. I believed God was up to something and presenting us a second chance. I searched high and low for letters and pictures that Lee sent me back in the day.

Mr. Recen Lee Divorced Part I

"Lomasi, if you find the letters, don't read them," Lee told me. "I want to read them to you when I come to Los Angeles."

"Okay, I won't," I promised. I continued to look through boxes and photo albums for these keepsakes.

As exciting as it was to have Lee back in my life, it also made me anxious. I didn't want to lose him again, and I definitely didn't want to hurt him again after hearing how disappointed he was when I aborted my plans to move to Atlanta. I wanted this to be an amazing and unforgettable trip for him, so I spent several days planning an itinerary.

Lee and I were both grinning ear to ear when I picked him up at the airport. We hit the ground running, visiting Venice Beach and sightseeing. I stopped by my house to grab the cards and pictures Lee had sent me years ago, and then we went to dinner and bowling. There was one question I hadn't been able to get off my mind.

"Why divorce? What happened?" I asked.

Lee explained that the lack of communication was the culprit, and that led to bitterness and a divide. He took responsibility for his part in the demise of the relationship. I thought that was honorable. He also shared what he learned from it, and how he was going to do things differently in the future.

"You guys didn't try to work it out?" I inquired.

"We went to counseling, but it was too far gone at that point."

I knew Lee had been married for several years. I couldn't understand why both parties didn't fight to save the relationship, but it wasn't my cross to bear. I can honestly say I fought for my marriage, and I wasn't married nearly half as long as he was. That led to my next question.

"Your divorce is fairly recent; do you think you're ready to date?" I probed.

I had been divorced for eighteen months and hadn't dated anyone. During the first year, I was too emotional. I got anxious just at the thought of giving someone my number, never mind going on a date. After what I'd been through with Mason, moving on too early was something I wasn't even considering.

I was adamant about healing. I didn't want to bring any baggage into the next relationship. I just didn't want to be hurt by Lee. Frankly, I had seen this movie before, and I was the lead actress. I knew how it would play out.

"Lomasi, if it was a few months ago, in the summer, then I probably wouldn't have been ready because I was still in the 'maybe' place. Maybe we will get back together. By September, I was already coming to terms with it all. If I met someone new, then I would say I probably wouldn't be ready, but with you … yes. I am ready. It's organic," he explained.

Mr. Recen Lee Divorced Part I

And here we were just a few months past September. I tried not to be doubtful, but that seed lingered. If I hadn't had great chemistry with him, I would've declined getting into a relationship. But, against my better judgment, I took the risk and lived in the moment.

The few days Lee spent in L.A. were amazing and unforgettable. We continued visiting landmarks, including the Hollywood sign, Hollywood Walk of Fame and Rodeo Drive in Beverly Hills. Lee actually surprised me and made reservations at Crustaceans in Beverly Hills. At dinner, I handed Lee the envelope with the cards I'd found and he started reading them. Written almost twenty-five years ago, they were romantic, sweet, and affectionate. I was filled with those "warm and fuzzies" again. I couldn't believe this man made me feel this way so soon. But why?

After Crustacean's, we went to The Room, a lounge in Hollywood. It was a small place, but we danced all night. Even though it was packed, it felt like we were the only two in there. Iit was another night of fun and bliss.

By the time Lee flew home, I really liked him a lot. The unknown frightened me and made me nervous. Lee was recently divorced, and I didn't know the role his

Unqualified: The Ineligible Bachelor

children's mother still played in his life. They had only been divorced about five months.

I thought Lee would need some time to grieve the loss and cut the emotional and perhaps physical ties. Truth be told, this is what unqualified him. It made me extremely anxious to be back in this place. Like I said, I had seen this movie before.

"Don't worry about anything; instead, pray about everything. Tell God what you need, and thank him for all he has done." (Philippians 4:6, NLT)

Ineligible Bachelor #9:
Mr. Recen Lee Divorced Part II

"Good evening, at this time we're going to begin our boarding process at this time. We'll now start preboarding customers with disabilities." The gate agent announced. "We now welcome our first class customers."

To celebrate New Year's, I flew to New York to meet Lee. He was going there for the holiday. I found it rather strange that he was going there because his children and their mother were going to visit her family members. I found the whole thing a little strange. His visit was supposed to be a surprise for his children.

I still was battling doubts about this relationship; it seemed the more I paid attention I had good reason to be anxious. One thing that bothered me was he and his ex-wife were business partners, or she worked for him. He didn't divulge this information to me. I figured it out from some photos and comments posted on his Facebook page. I didn't understand why he hadn't mentioned it; I found that to be a little shady. He once told me he was an open book. From what I was observing, he was more like a book ajar.

We had a great time ringing in the new year, dancing, eating great food, and just enjoying being together. Toward the end of my stay, I started coughing and having asthma complications. We found a teahouse and I ordered some Mullein tea to soothe my throat and lungs. Lee had some of that exact tea shipped to me at home in L.A. to enjoy while I recovered. He made me feel very special.

Two weeks later, Lee invited me to Atlanta to stay with him for a few days. He also invited my stepdad, Chris, and me to an Atlanta Hawks basketball game. He was a season ticket holder. *Wow, he wants to invite my stepdad and son? Where could this be heading?* I wasn't thinking marriage or anything. It was too soon for all that, but I felt like I was living out a fairytale.

Not to mention Lee had been making comments about my moving to Atlanta. I wasn't in love with him, but I knew I cared about him a lot, and those feelings grew by the minute—right alongside the anxiety. We were at dinner one night during my visit when we had a deep conversation.

"What is the one thing you fear with us?" I asked him.

"That's a great question," he responded. "Not being able to make you happy."

I know what you're thinking: "Aww, that is so sweet." Nope. That's not what I thought. In fact, it concerned me. It spoke to my anxiety, the part that feared the unknown with this newly single man and father. *Why would he say that?* I asked myself. *Does he know something about himself that would make him think he was going to make me unhappy?* Now I was even more uneasy, but I set my fears aside and enjoyed our amazing time together.

We weren't able to be together on Valentine's Day and that was especially hard. However, we sent each other thoughtful gifts. I could tell Lee really paid attention to the things I shared with him. I missed him a lot.

His birthday was coming up in a couple of weeks, so I told him I wanted to visit to celebrate the occasion. He told me the best dates to come, so I made arrangements to arrive in Atlanta on a Thursday morning and depart Monday afternoon. I told Lee we could plan to do something special Thursday or Sunday. That's when he told me we'd have to get together Sunday because his friends were taking him out Thursday and Saturday.

So, that meant during my four-day visit, I would see him Friday and Sunday. *What the heck?! Is he serious?!* I asked him if what he had planned was a "guys" thing and he said it was. I was beginning to think my visit wasn't such a good idea. I was hurt and furious, so I let him have it.

"Masi B., I didn't think it would be a big deal since you know a lot of people. I thought maybe you'd want to go visit them and spend time with them, and then I'd do my thing with the guys," he explained.

"Lee, I'm taking days off from work to come see you, not other people," I retorted. "I'll see my stepdad and son of course, but my sole purpose for coming to Atlanta this trip is you. I could see if it was one day with the guys, but two of the four nights that I'm going to be there? I don't know about that."

I thought back to that conversation when he said he feared not being able to make me happy. *Was this what he was talking about?*

"I don't know what to say. The plans were already made a while ago," Lee said.

Wow! So shady! How did we get here? was all I could think about. This from the guy who told me "I'm always available for you" and I'll always put you first." I was so disappointed in him. And for the first time, I felt cold toward him. I wasn't sure who this man was—because he wasn't the Lee I knew.

Mr. Recen Lee Divorced Part II

"Lee, I'm going to cancel my trip. We can do it another time." He had proven what his priorities were, and I wasn't one of them.

About a half hour later, Lee texted and told me not to cancel my trip. He was going to cancel Thursday with the guys. He said he didn't want to miss an opportunity to see me. Lee redeemed himself.

I arrived in Atlanta Thursday as planned. I was so happy to see him and spend time with him again. He took me to an escape room one night (no, we didn't make it out in sixty minutes!), and we saw a romantic movie at the theater. The "warm and fuzzies" were back, and all I could think about was the potential for our own love story.

Something profound occurred in our relationship that night. It brings tears to my eyes now to say it—not because of what happened but the aftermath. Lee and I had sex. I had abstained from sex for the majority of my relationships after having my son. The only time I didn't was when I was so angry and bitter with God after my first marriage to Earl. I purposefully did everything opposite of God's word.

The sexual event between Lee and me wasn't love, it was more lust. Maybe blame it on the alcohol, I don't know. Regardless, love was definitely missing. My emotions got the best of me, and his needs got the best of him. My soul didn't feel good afterward. I understood how Adam and Eve felt when they ate the apple in the Garden of Eden.

I felt exposed and impure. There was nothing about me that felt special and cherished. It was like I was outside of my body. I no longer felt like the apple of God's eye and surely not Lee's. *Father God, please forgive me,* I prayed silently as tears streamed down my face.

The next couple of days were awkward. Lee was still attentive, and we had a great time when we went to a club, but our chemistry was off. I was nervous and anxious. When we were at his house, he didn't seem to be comfortable around me and would hide out in his office. It reminded me of when Adam hid himself from God because of his shame.

The day of his birthday shindig, I barely saw Lee. He left early in the morning and stayed gone most of the day. I ended up going out with one of my old college friends. The energy continued to shift, and not in a good way. I even had a dream that this would be the last weekend I'd ever see or talk to Lee again.

Mr. Recen Lee Divorced Part II

The next night I took Lee to a restaurant for his birthday and it was awful. We barely had any conversation, and the mood was heavy. It was like pulling teeth to get him to talk. That wasn't like us. At one point I asked him to address the elephant in the room, but he acted like he didn't know what I was talking about. He blamed his mood on being hung over from his birthday event with the guys. The next day he took me to the airport, kissed me goodbye, and drove off.

That was the last time I saw Lee; I was devastated. He jilted me. I never imagined he could do something like that, especially given our friendship and history. It was a tough loss and I grieved hard.

It wasn't just the few months of our blissful time together, but the twenty-plus years of friendship and all the "what ifs" I asked myself in between. I was also grieving the loss of a special friend I had held dear in my heart from day one.

I had to ask myself an honest question: *Did you love him, Lomasi?* The truthful answer was, I did. I already loved him as a friend, but I had started falling in love with him and the "happily ever after" fairytale that seemed to be within reach. I stepped out on faith, pushed past the anxieties, and stayed in prayer. This loss hurt, and it hurt a lot.

About three weeks later, God spoke to me while I was napping on the couch. He told me Lee just wasn't ready, although he adored me. He wanted more, but he couldn't now. God assured me I did everything right. I had loved Lee, and I was genuine.

Then he led me to Matthew 18:15: "If another believer sins against you, go privately and point out the offense. If the other person listens and confesses it, you have won that person back." *Do you want me to call him, God, and tell him what he has done to me?* I questioned. God gave me the strength to call Lee and we had a nice, lengthy conversation later that night.

He explained what he was going through and the struggles he was having. Lee said it was his first sexual encounter since his divorce. It was mine, too, since Mason. He felt it should've been special, and he felt horrible about that. Lee didn't know how to process what he was feeling, let alone how to communicate it.

I don't know if it was BS or the truth, but I identified with what he was saying. When Lee and I first reconnected, I felt like I was cheating on Mason, even though we were divorced. I felt like I needed to tell Mason I was taking a chance and moving on. So, I understood what Lee was saying.

Even though Lee and I talked from time to time after that, our dating relationship ended. Lee was unqualified. It was what I knew all along and feared the most: he wasn't ready to be in a relationship. God's talk with me and Lee's explanation was the closure I needed.

I enjoyed our time together. I don't know if there will be anything more down the line, but the friendship was restored and I'm grateful for that. I'll admit, I missed being with Lee, but the worry and anxiety were a lot to bear. I refuse to live like that again; I will continue to fight for and maintain my peace.

As I said in the beginning, "I am a treasure!" The word of God says, "The man who **finds** a wife, finds a **treasure,** and he receives favor from the Lord." (Proverbs 18:22, NLT) A treasure is meant only for the one who is qualified to find it. Lee tried to hunt for the treasure, but he wasn't equipped. He couldn't see and appreciate me the way God intended.

The word of God says I am more precious than rubies. "Who can find a virtuous and capable wife? She is more precious than rubies." (Proverbs 31:10, NLT) Many men refer to themselves as kings. Long ago, a king identified the value of rubies by their color. He knew the darkest red was the highest value.

I AM WORTH MORE THAN RUBIES. And God, if you call me capable (qualified), then I know you have a man qualified for me! I will continue to wait on the King to send my king—because a true king knows the value of his ruby.

Unqualified: The Ineligible Bachelor

"Truthful words stand the test of time, but lies are soon exposed." (Proverbs 12:19, NLT)

"... Forget about what's happened; don't keep going over old history. Be alert, be present. I'm about to do something brand new ..." (Isaiah 43:18-19, MSG)

"The man who **finds** a wife, finds a **treasure,** and he receives favor from the Lord." (Proverbs 18:22, NLT)

"Who can find a virtuous and capable wife? She is more precious than rubies." (Proverbs 31:10, NLT)

Epilogue

Bing! The Facebook Messenger notification alerted, and I looked to see who was sending me a message.

"Long time no see. I'm happy to see you're doing well."

I looked at the name, but I couldn't connect the name to the face. The gentleman, dressed in a designer suit, was wearing glasses with dark lenses in the picture. The name read Evan. *Who the heck is this?*

"Hey, I mean no disrespect and please forgive me, but how do we know each other?" I typed back.

"None taken. You never knew my real name?" LOL

"It's Snug!" he replied.

"Hey! Oh, wow! How are you? Yes, it's been a very long time!"

"Lomasi, I never thought we'd have the opportunity to talk again. I'm still me; however, I'm grown—a real man and very successful. Sometimes I wonder what could've been. You know? I mean, I never gave you what you deserved when we were younger," Evan confessed.

"Snu-" I cut myself off. "I'm sorry, Evan. I know you as Snug. That was your name when we were kids. May I call you that?"

"Sure. My family still calls me that."

Unqualified: The Ineligible Bachelor

"Snug, I definitely didn't think we'd talk or ever see each other again either. And how could you have possibly given me the "grown-man treatment" when we were teenagers?"

"Can I call you, so I can hear your voice?" Evan asked.

"Sure!" I responded, as I opened the door to another opportunity of what would turn out to be another unqualified candidate: Mr. Nine D. Percent, aka Evan Willis, aka Snug—my first boyfriend, first love, and the one to whom I lost my virginity.

After reconnecting with Evan, three years passed with no further communication. I had just relocated from Los Angeles to Atlanta during the COVID-19 pandemic. What started as a simple question from my son eight months earlier had become my reality: a new beginning in a new state and a new job.

I just happened to be on Facebook a month after moving and saw that Evan had liked a story I had created. *Hmm, that's interesting. Where's he been?* I hadn't seen him much on Facebook during the three previous years and not at all in the past few months. I decided to say hello.

"Hey! Long time no chat. How's it going?" I messaged.

"Hi, Lomasi. It's been a while. How are you doing?" Evan replied.

"I'm doing well! I relocated to the Atlanta area a few weeks ago, so I'm just trying to get settled." I knew Evan had lived in Atlanta for about twenty years—nearly the same length of time I had lived in Los Angeles.

"Oh, wow! I need to come see you then. Are you staying in the "A" permanently, or is it just for a little while?" he inquired.

Epilogue

Bling. Evan's cell phone number popped up next.

"I have separated from my wife recently, and I got my own place until we figure out the next steps," he added.

I knew he was married based on his Facebook photos. He had confided in me during our phone conversation several years earlier that he and his wife were having marital problems. He was leaning toward divorce due to the toxicity in the marriage and home. At the time, I suggested to him they should try marital counseling.

Evan continued our conversation and shared tragic news about the passing of his oldest child. Then he dropped another bombshell that one of his younger children had been diagnosed with cancer. I was speechless. My heart went out to him, and I told him I would lift his child up in prayer.

I suggested he take his time making any decisions regarding his marriage. I asked him if he prayed and talked to God about what was on his plate, his emotions, and his questions. He told me he lost faith when he tragically lost his oldest child. I encouraged him and reminded him that God is still working, regardless of how things looked.

"Hey, let me know when we can grab lunch or something," he said, switching gears. "I'd love to see you for the first time since we were teenagers!"

We had dinner about a week later, and it was surreal meeting up with him after thirty years. He looked pretty much the same, but a grown and distinguished version. I was nervous at first; I mean how many people get the opportunity to reconnect with their very first boyfriend and love? We shared stories about our lives over the years and just had a really good time. There was a purpose in our reconnection, but I wasn't quite sure what that was.

Unqualified: The Ineligible Bachelor

"Lomasi, I really enjoyed dinner with you. I want to make up for the thirty years we lost."

"Hey, Snug. Thank you so much for dinner. I really enjoyed myself as well. And there's nothing to make up for, friend. I am glad we reconnected, and we can remain friends—but I have a lot of respect for what you and your family are going through. That said, I will be keeping appropriate boundaries."

"I don't know. Hearing your voice and seeing you smile makes me feel good," he expressed.

Evan and I continued to talk, text, and hang out over the next month or two. Though I didn't ask him to, he kept me in the loop about all his divorce proceedings. When I told him to stop sharing, he claimed he wanted me to know.

"My divorce is like ninety percent done," Evan proclaimed one day.

"Oh, really? Ninety percent? How in the hell did you come up with that random number, Snug? Is there some divorce meter I don't know about?" I asked jokingly. He must have forgotten I had already been there and done that. I had never seen a divorce finish in less than six months.

"I can't wait to show off my real wife!" he exclaimed, confidently.

"What!? Your real wife? I am keeping myself in the friend zone, sir," I reminded him.

"Lomasi, I'm not letting you get away again. I apologize if I'm being forward, but I'm serious. I think it's meant to be. Maybe I'm tripping, but I haven't felt this strong about something in my whole life. There are so many

Epilogue

places and things I want to experience with you. We'll be busy forever."

"Well, Snug, if it's meant to be, it will be. Just take your time to do what you need to do for yourself. Divorce is not easy." I encouraged him to continue healing and handling his business.

We continued our friendship, which was platonic; however, emotionally we were connecting. Evan even gave me a key to his house in case I needed a pit stop to rest on my ninety-minute commute from work. One of the cool things we did was read and complete a Bible devotional together. He hung out with my dad (who did a lot for him when we were teenagers) and me a couple of times. He would bring food over and we would all play cards (Spades). He continued to keep me in the loop about his divorce that was "ninety percent" done.

Then one day he told me the upcoming court date, which would take place in about a month's time. *I guess this is really happening,* I told myself. Mr. Nine D. Percent was trying to prove he was qualified every chance he got. And that's when I started to let my guard down—a little. BAD MISTAKE.

Scriptures

- "For everything there is a season, a time for every activity under heaven…. time to embrace and a time to turn away …" (Ecclesiastes 3:1, 5, NLT)

- "No, dear brothers and sisters, I have not achieved it, but I focus on this one thing: Forgetting the past and looking forward to what lies ahead." (Philippians 3:13, NLT)

- "In the same way, you husbands must give honor to your wives. Treat your wife with understanding as you live together. She may be weaker than you are, but she is your equal partner in God's gift of new life. Treat her as you should so your prayers will not be hindered." (1 Peter 3:7, NLT)

- "For I know the plans I have for you," says the Lord. "They are plans for good and not for disaster, to give you a future and a hope." (Jeremiah 29:11, NLT)

Unqualified: The Ineligible Bachelor

- "Don't team up with those who are unbelievers. How can righteousness be a partner with wickedness? How can light live with darkness?" (2 Corinthian 6:14, NLT)

- "Wait on the Lord; be of good courage, And He shall strengthen your heart; Wait, I say, on the Lord!" (Psalm 27:14, NKJV)

- "But those who wait on the Lord shall renew their strength; they shall mount up with wings like eagles, they shall run and not be weary, they shall walk and not faint." (Isaiah 40:31, NKJV)

- "First pride, then the crash—the bigger the ego, the harder the fall." (Proverbs 16:18, MSG)

- "For you know when your faith is tested, your endurance has a chance to grow." (James 1:3, NLT)

- "The spirit of the sovereign LORD is on me, because the LORD has anointed me to proclaim good news to the poor. He has sent me to bind up the brokenhearted, to proclaim freedom for the captives and release from darkness for the prisoners." (Isaiah 61:1, NIV)

Scriptures

- "It is not good for man to be alone. I will make a helper who is suitable for him." (Genesis 2:18, NLT)

- "Who can find a virtuous wife? For her worth is far above rubies." (Proverbs 31:10, NKJV)

- "Don't worry about anything; instead, pray about everything. Tell God what you need and thank him for all he has done." (Philippians 4:6, NLT)

- "Truthful words stand the test of time, but lies are soon exposed." (Proverbs 12:19, NLT)

- "If another believer sins against you, go privately and point out the offense. If the person listens and confesses it, you have won that person back. (Matthew 18: 15)

- "… Forget about what's happened; don't keep going over old history. Be alert, be present. I'm about to do something brand new…." (Isaiah 43:18-19, MSG)

- "The man who finds a wife finds a treasure, and he receives favor from the Lord." (Proverbs 18:22, NLT)

Self Reflection

Reflect on your relationship(s) to determine if there is a qualified or unqualified bachelor in your life. Know your worth. You are a treasure worth finding. Don't be afraid to let go and wait. Finally, pray and ask God to send you the king who is qualified for you, because He says "Your worth is far above rubies ..." As I said earlier, long ago only a king identified the value of rubies by their color. He knew the darkest color red was the most valuable. Your king will know your value the moment he sees you.

Notes

Notes

Notes

Made in the USA
Columbia, SC
21 September 2023